Brass Bands and New Orleans Jazz

The street bands *marched into the 1970s. A ballyhoo parade in the French Quarter, 1974, with the Olympia Brass Band. Note the revived uniforms, patterned on turn-of-the-century brass-band garb.*

BRASS BANDS
and New Orleans Jazz

WILLIAM J. SCHAFER
with assistance from Richard B. Allen

LOUISIANA STATE UNIVERSITY PRESS *Baton Rouge and London*

Copyright © 1977 by Louisiana State University Press
All rights reserved
Manufactured in the United States of America

Designer: Dwight Agner
Type face: VIP Aster
Typesetter: Graphic World, Inc., St. Louis, Missouri
Printer and binder: Kingsport Press, Inc., Kingsport, Tennessee

LIBRARY OF CONGRESS CATALOGING IN PUBLICATION DATA

Schafer, William John, 1937–
  Brass bands and New Orleans jazz.

  Bibliography: p.
  Discography:
  Includes index.
  1. Bands (Music)—Louisiana—New Orleans. 2. Jazz music—
Louisiana—New Orleans. I. Allen, Richard B., joint author. II. Title.
ML1311.7.L7S3   785'.06'720976335   76–58469
ISBN 0–8071–0280–6
ISBN 0–8071–0282–2 pbk.

Contents

Illustrations

Preface and Acknowledgments

THIS BOOK BEGAN as an attempt to use the materials in the William Ransom Hogan Jazz Archive in the Howard-Tilton Memorial Library, Tulane University, for research. I concentrated especially on the enormously rich lode of oral biography and interview material in the collection. My first debt is to Richard B. Allen, curator of the jazz archive, who aided in every step of the research and writing and who took time from his busy schedule to write material for the book and locate many sources of information. I wish also to thank former curator William Russell, who has spent his life collecting and preserving materials for study of New Orleans music. His photographs, observations from his *Notes*, and statements from his writings are central to this work. For permission to reproduce photographs, I wish to thank Mike Casimir, Richard A. Hubsch, F. Jack Hurley, William Russell, and Bernard M. Steinau. Their visual materials are an important dimension of this book.

My thanks also go to Berea College and its Committee for Professional Growth, which awarded me grants to research and write this book. The college has been patient and encouraging throughout the process. Other members of the college faculty and administration who have given me moral support and much-needed academic stimulation over the years are too numerous to list individually. To them, I offer my personal thanks for their collective aid.

As with any work relying on oral history, there are unconfirmed opinions in many of the statements I have quoted from older musicians and observers of New Orleans music. Sometimes the observers contradict each other and themselves; sometimes their memories of a half-century of music-making and listening are distorted. But I felt their own words on the music of New Orleans communicated something unique, and I have thus consistently relied on their testimony and their idioms. I believe their expression of the meaning and feeling of their music is an important dimension in the study of jazz and its origins.

Brass Bands and New Orleans Jazz

Chapter I What the Brass Band Played

Ragtime music was made-up stuff . . . didn't have no ragtime written. Had marches, mazurkas, polkas, schottische, quadrille—all that was music, you see. Well, all bands played that.
　　　　　　　　—Willie Parker, interviewed April 29, 1960

FROM 1880 TO 1910 was—to alloy a metaphor—the golden age of the brass band in America. Until his death in 1892, Patrick Gilmore was the unchallenged king of American band music. His tours, his first-rate concert band, and the extravaganzas he staged founded the modern wind-band tradition in America.[1]

The development of the modern wind band often parallels the growth of instrumental technology and the perfection of modern wind instruments. When we speak of a military band or a brass band or, in more recent usage, a wind ensemble, we refer to an instrumental group composed of brass instruments, woodwinds, and percussion. The history starts, basically, with the creation of military music groups accompanying armies in the counterreformation wars of seventeenth-century Europe and England. Musicians playing natural trumpets and horns, fifes or flute-related woodwinds, oboes, bassoons, accompanied by miscellaneous percussion, provided armies with cheerful marching music. Through the next century this impromptu musical group became a by-product of military life. By the time of the American Revolution, musical groups of every size were part of military organization.

In the late eighteenth century a fad for "Turkish music" refined burgeoning military music patterns. The importation of Turkish (*i.e.*, Middle-Eastern) percussion—snare drums, cymbals, large bass drums, triangles and the formation of drum corps using these instruments established drumming centrally in military music.[2] The Turkish music fad is reflected in such standard classical works as Mozart's keyboard imitation in his *Rondo a la Turka*; in Haydn's *Military* Symphony (no. 100), with its use of the military percussion section; in Beethoven's "Turkish March" from *The Ruins of Athens*; and even in episodes in the fourth movement of the Ninth Symphony, when the "Ode to Joy" turns into a village band march, complete with syncopated percussion parts for big drum, cymbals, and triangle. Other band instruments available at the time included simple fifes, oboes, clarinets, flutes, trombones, and some early "brass" instruments (*i.e.*, instruments using metal cup-shaped mouthpieces), ancestors of the modern trumpet/cornet, plus curiosities like the serpent and flageolet.[3] These bands were primitive, but their influence was broad, as is reflected in the wind suites and marches of Haydn, Mozart, C. P. E. Bach, and their contemporaries. The wind band was a common musical resource in Europe and America.

During this time in America, wind music was fostered by groups like the Moravians, who continued high-baroque traditions of brass playing in religious works.[4] It was also a military tradition incorporated by the early revolutionary militia and army units. Technology improved wind instruments, especially woodwinds. The modern clarinet and transverse flute developed through the eighteenth century, as instrument-makers improved intonation and simplified fingering. By the beginning of the nineteenth century a demand for wind groups existed in America, and instrument-builders devised tools necessary for players.

In the first quarter of the nineteenth century new forms of military music evolved. The development of the keyed bugle led to ensembles featuring this instrument. The keyed bugle was an ophicleide, a bugle-shaped brass instrument with a cup-shaped mouthpiece, equipped with keyed holes in the tubing, like those of a saxophone. It was difficult to play well, hard to keep in tune with itself and other instruments, and fairly fragile. But it produced a piercing, stirring tone like the natural trumpet or military bugle and was capable of playing complex music. Bugle virtuosi mastered the instrument, and through the period of the Mexican War bugle bands replaced the old fife-and-drum corps and miscellaneous bands dating back to the Revolution. The sound of brass became, in this generation, ineradicably associated with military music.

By the 1840s another technological development in instrument design had replaced the unreliable keyed bugles and other ophicleides with instruments easier to play and more uniform in pitch and intonation. Members of a "family" of related horns using piston or rotary valves and shaped with a consistent conical bore (internal diameter) from mouthpiece to bell, these brass instruments were known under the general rubric of saxhorns, after inventor Adolphe Sax. They could be assembled into a self-consistent wind group, augmented by woodwinds and/or percussion, and a military band was thus formed. These instruments were disseminated by New York musical entrepreneur Allen Dodworth, who formed a first-rate band and hawked the instruments throughout America. By the 1850s the saxhorn family was the standard brass-band complement. [5] Some of these horns were peculiar in that, unlike modern brasses, they were designed to be aimed *back* across the player's shoulder with the bell pointing to the rear.[6] This design feature was a holdover from the eighteenth-century practice of heading troops with a band. The horns threw the music back to the following troops, but they made the instruments impractical except on the march. Despite such limitations the saxhorn family was quickly accepted: "By mid-century the cornet had all but entirely replaced the older keyed bugle as the leading melodic instrument in American bands. The lower clapper-keyed ophicleides were replaced variously with Sax's rotary or piston-valved alto, tenor, baritone and bass horns, and many bands changed their names from 'Bugle Band' to 'Cornet Band,' thus calling attention to their new instruments."[7] At the time of the Civil War the new brass instruments were in universal use.

The Civil War further disseminated bands in America. Players were trained on piston-valve instruments of conical bore, and the instruments were widely available. Many bands were formed or recruited intact during the war;[8] and following the war the band tradition continued, stimulated by former-army bandmasters like Patrick Gilmore or Claudio Grafulla, who led civilian bands of great brilliance. Through the last quarter of the century civilian and military-connected bands developed, and there was even further refinement in instrument technology. Woodwinds were used more in conjunction with brasses. The clumsy backward-pointing saxhorns were superseded by upright and forward-aimed cornets, alto horns, tenor horns, baritone horns, and helicons or tubas. Trombones were added to the brass choir—valve trombones at first, then the slide trombone, which has persisted since the Middle Ages as one of the oldest brasses.[9] Older conical-bore instruments were often replaced by instruments with a cylindrical bore—not a uniform taper from mouthpiece to bell, but a flaring at the end of the long brass wind-column, as in the modern trumpet. Continued technological development led to improved piston-cylinder valves replacing older string-activated rotary valves. Greater precision of tubing and fittings was possible, and intonation-pitch problems were conquered.

The first New Orleans street band on phonograph records—*Bunk's Brass Band, May, 1945. Left to right: Bunk Johnson, "Kid Shots" Madison, Isidore Barbarin, Adolphe Alexander, Sr., Lawrence Marrero, George Lewis, Warren "Baby" Dodds, Jim Robinson, Joseph "Red" Clark.*

By the turn of the century village bands flourished across America, and traveling virtuoso bands like those of Sousa, T. P. Brooke, and others (all patterned on the phenomenally successful bands of Patrick Gilmore in the 1880s) supplied magnificent examples of the spectrum of music possible with a wind group. Instruments were inexpensive and there was a broad popular movement toward bands and band music.[10]

The pattern for forming a village band was similar across the country. It was usually assembled of amateur players, often with military-band experience, tutored by the local musician with the most brass expertise. Frequently volunteers had no musical experience, but they had a strong desire to don a fancy frog-fastened coat and peaked cap and carry a shiny horn in local parades. The musicians were taught from scratch and probably never attained much technical polish. Teachers might have used various *solfege* ("sight-singing") methods to teach the rudiments of music reading. Wind and band "method" books were published to aid the student. But the usual pattern was for a bandmaster to rehearse his group regularly, working by sections and with individual players in the ensemble, but rehearsing the entire band rather than offering private lessons or tutoring. The band must have been viewed as a homogeneous instrumental choir, not a collection of individual musical experts.

A typical provincial band in the last decades of the nineteenth century was something like this model:

The Brass Band of Glenville, N.Y. . . . was organized in 1876 and was comprised of ten players, equipped as follows:

> 2 E^b cornets
> 2 B^b cornets
> 1 B^b valve trombone
> 2 B^b alto [horns]
> 1 B^b tenor [horn]
> 1 B^b baritone [horn]
> 1 E^b bass tuba

. . . After a few years drums and cymbals were added, as well as a B^b helicon bass and a B^b fluegelhorn.[11]

This was a true brass band, and all-brass ensembles dominated until improved woodwind systems made flutes, clarinets, and similar instruments more accessible for the amateur player. By the last decade of the century *brass band* would mean an ensemble of mixed brasses, reeds, and percussion; and larger concert bands would be dominated proportionately in number by reeds.

The first important impact of brass bands on jazz was through instrumentation, with an emphasis on brass instruments, polyphonic musical style, and sectional playing within the band. Instruments favored by band musicians were those manufactured for military bands, designed for outdoor playing, of large bore and generally with larger mouthpieces than instruments used by symphonic musicians. They were built to produce a *loud*, carrying tone, and they were designed as part of a family of instruments combined in sections of a band.

Against this background of the development of the brass band or silver cornet band of nineteenth-century America is the parallel history of brass bands in New Orleans, with their Afro-American adaptation of the tradition. To explore the synthesis of the broad black American heritage with the wind-band tradition, one must plunge into the vortex where these two rivers of American music meet and thereby discover the unique art of the New Orleans street bands.

In discussions of American music, especially the music of black Americans, much confusion has been created. Writers on the subject have invented a large category and arbitrarily defined it as "jazz"; and we have divided and subdivided this category by chronology, geography, and esthetics. Common sense rebels against this. Eddie Condon said, "We called it music." William Russell settled for plain American music. Louis Armstrong said that if you didn't know what it was when you heard it he couldn't explain it to you. These are not just quips or naive oversimplifications. The street bands of New Orleans, and their music, are a case in point: do we settle for "jazz" and let the nuances and details go? or can we view this unique phenomenon without conventional categories and classifications? How can we talk about music that encompasses different genres and transcends traditional categorization?

What is to be made of the Eureka Brass Band, which from the 1920s to the 1950s habitually read from scores standard marches like "Our Director" and standard funeral dirges like "Fallen Heroes" and which also played freely developed "head" arrangements (including solos, sophisticated section-work, duo, trio, and quartet improvisational passages against ensemble counterpoint) of jazz numbers like "Panama," "Whoopin' Blues," and "Lady Be Good"? Or of the E. Gibson Brass Band, which played a pastiche-march —"The Little Rascal"—freely constructed from the trio of Sousa's "The Thunderer" and bits and pieces of old pop tunes? Or of the Olympia Brass Band, which read standard marches like Frank A. Panella's "On the Square" in parades and also played jazz standards? If the Eureka band played jazz in "Panama," what do we call its reading of the dirge "Eternity"? When the Young Tuxedo Brass Band played a hymn-medley, was it playing jazz, or was this church or military music?

These are not scholastic quibbles. If we *begin* by assuming that the brass bands of New Orleans from 1890 to 1970 have been basically jazz groups, we will reach narrow conclusions about what we hear them play. We will hear jazz everywhere and assume that jazz practices, as we understand them, apply to everything. If, instead, we can begin naively, assuming that these are "bands of music" in the oldest, simplest sense, that the black New Orleans musicians in the Onward Brass Band, the Excelsior Brass Band, the Eureka Brass Band were bandsmen like those in hundreds of other village or municipal bands across America, we can listen freshly and may hear surprising things.

For the old American impulse to form a brass band and join a parade is where the tradition begins. It reaches back to the nineteenth-century genesis of a school of native wind music and musicians, perhaps the broadest American instrumental tradition. The black New Orleans musicians who formed and joined brass bands in the decades following the Civil War were stepping with the parade of American musical life in their century—a movement that had already produced Patrick Gilmore as its reigning native genius, that had intrigued Louis Moreau Gottschalk, that would culminate in the quintessentially American music of John Philip Sousa. Through the century literature for the wind band—including martial, religious, dance, and light classical music of many varieties—swelled and developed, and the sophistication of the bands themselves rapidly increased. The story of brass bands begins, then, before jazz, and it runs a course separate from the stream of jazz—parallel and often contiguous, but never identical. To see how these two powerful American musical inventions ultimately mingled, we must trace the channels of both.

The brass band in nineteenth-century America was as ubiquitous in its time as are jukeboxes and electronic music systems in ours. When even large cities could not raise a symphony orchestra, every village had its silver cornet band and bandstand in the square.[12] Brass bands played for circuses, carnivals, minstrel and medicine shows, political rallies, churches, picnics, dances, athletic contests, holiday gatherings. The Salvation Army employed the small brass band as a potent weapon in its evangelistic crusade, and politicians and pitchmen of every stamp used brass bands for ballyhoo. Every military troop, quasimilitary drill team, volunteer fire squad, lodge, or social club had its auxiliary band to swell holiday pageantry. Every crossroads village hankered to form a "splendid brass band" to head seasonal parades and to serenade fairs and reunions.

In New Orleans the brass band was a powerful influence on the new jazz music that developed around 1900. Brass bands gave jazz its instrumentation, its instrumental techniques, its basic repertoire. Habits and attitudes of brass bandsmen carried into jazz, shaping its music for decades after it was apparently dissociated from the military tradition. The influence of the brass bands in early jazz is omnipresent. To understand jazz, we must begin with its roots, and the taproot of the tradition is the nineteenth-century brass band. It is an irony of history that New Orleans street bands were not recorded until a full generation after their initial impact on jazz and popular music. But even so, phonograph recordings do not constitute a complete history of jazz.

If we look carefully at early New Orleans music in its milieu and time, the brass band emerges as a major source, a gene pool, for jazz. It contributed more to jazz than can be easily calculated. But the bands also have a distinct history and separate traditions. To do justice to a legion of musicians who built the tradition of street bands, we must examine what they sought and what they accomplished. An overview begins with a report from 1878, by one of the first observers of the black music milieu after the Civil War:

New Orleans has several fine brass bands among its colored population. "Kelly's Band" and the "St. Bernard" deserve particular mention here. The "St. Bernard" is composed of a very intelligent class of young men, studious, and of excellent moral character; in fact, they form a splendid corps of musicians, excelled by none. With these two bands and some others, the names of which I have not now at hand, the people of New Orleans are always well supplied with the best of martial music.[13]

Or we can look at another landmark in the early history of the bands, the appearance of the Excelsior Brass Band at the New Orleans Cotton States Exposition of 1885, for the formal opening of the Colored People's Exhibit. This band—already widely known as the finest black brass band in the city and veterans of tours of northern cities—played marches, a medley entitled "The Rapid Transit Around the World," and a waltz. The reporter present called one performance a "stirring piece of music."[14] From this time on, we can follow the stories of the brass bands of New Orleans that eventually became more famous, perhaps ironically, as footnotes in jazz history.

Problems in semantics arise immediately, however, since over the years commentators and musicians have multiplied and confused terminology. More recently, musicologists and cultural historians have compounded the confusion. First there is the terminology for wind-music groups. I have used *brass band* or *street band* interchangeably to refer to the small, basically brass-equipped New Orleans marching bands. Historically, the terms *brass band*, *military band*, and *marching band* have referred indiscriminately in America to any wind-percussion group playing marches. Rather than become entangled in pedantries, I have accepted this historical looseness. I prefer this to labeling the New Orleans groups *jazz bands*, or even something like *hot brass bands*, since it is important to view the groups as multifunctional bands playing straight scored music as well as improvisational pieces.

The second semantic knot is in the terminology for syncopated, improvisational music itself. Early musicians in New Orleans used the term *ragtime* as a catch-all for this new music ("new" *ca.* 1900), and they also described the new music with words like *ratty*, meaning low-down, or illegitimate by conventional standards. Other terms, like *barrelhouse*, *in the alley*, *faking*, or *head music*, occur. They all refer to the same unscored, impromptu music—Afro-American in texture, rhythm, and feeling. Although I have quoted many early musicians on this point, in order to show their own phraseology and ideas, I have preferred the term *ragtime*, as used in the early days, since it recalls the period context of the music.

The next problem is with the meaning of *jazz* and the influence of brass-band music on it. Without becoming enmeshed in the complexities of the term, we can assume that the word *jazz*, as used herein, is a syncopated, improvisational, Afro-American musical style developed in New Orleans from 1890 to 1915. This characteristic vernacular music drew on many sources, and the main impact of band music on it was in strengthening its beat—providing a tension between the march's strong, striding 1-and-3 beat emphasis and the Afro-American penchant for 2-and-4 accents. Gunther Schuller calls this a "basic bimetric approach," and band music, along with the march-shaped patterns of piano ragtime, was a primary source for this powerful double-forward motion.[15] The multithematic structure of the march, coupled with ragtime, gave early jazz a convenient formal basis. And the polyphonic formula of band scoring was crucial in conventionalizing instrumentation in early jazz. All these influences coincided with other cultural forces, but they were most accessible to New Orleans' black musicians through the medium of the small brass band.

Distinctions between music and ideas originated by black and white musicians in New Orleans offer the last semantic hurdle. Again it becomes very confusing, often hopelessly speculative, to repeatedly distinguish between musicians and bands on racial lines. I have generally referred to the street bands as *black*, because this is the hub of the tradition. Many excellent white bands and bandsmen contributed to the movement, but its essential character derived from black inspirations, from characteristic black musical techniques and practices, and from the deep fountain of black art in nineteenth-century America. Other terms could be substituted (*Afro-American*, for example), but again I have opted for a simple term used by the musicians. Some controversy is inevitable in dealing with oral history, with uncertain sources for ideas and data, but I have tried to keep terminology simple and direct, and to offer notes on questionable points. Some of this history is hidden from us, probably forever, but what remains is an important and singular chapter in our national musical heritage.

A great cosmopolitan city since the early nineteenth century, New Orleans flourished on music made by residents, amateur and professional. Opera, chamber music, all the cultivated musical forms were nurtured and displayed in profusion.[16] During the Civil War both northern and southern bands were quartered in the city and held parades and concerts. After the war instruments and teachers were readily available to aspiring musicians. A year-round demand for bands existed, and a long tradition of public ceremony was central to social life. The climate made outdoor events possible almost every day of the year; New Orleans was always ready for a picnic, parade, excursion, dance, any public ritual. Church festivals and processions and public holidays were abundant. It seems inevitable that bands should have formed to celebrate this rich social life.

Photo from Frank Rauscher, *Music on the March*

A typical Civil War regimental band—*of the 114th Pennsylvania
Volunteers—that served from 1862 to 1865. Note the Zouave dress and
the instrumentation, the over-the-shoulder saxhorn complement for
this average sixteen-piece band of the era.*

The Reconstruction period (1865–1877) was crucial in New Orleans, as throughout the South, for black people and their future. At this time a brass-band tradition was firmly rooted in the black community. During a decade of intense social and political turmoil and revision, hopes were high for a genuine egalitarian society in which black Americans would share in a reunited America's plenteous prospects. In New Orleans more than elsewhere in the South, there existed a large population of black citizens of high education and attainments, a society of freedmen dating back into the eighteenth century. These men led Reconstruction governments, and advice from one of the most famous of them, P. B. S. Pinchback, lieutenant-governor and acting governor of Louisiana (1872/73), reflects on the social situation of the time and its relation to groups that formed and sponsored early black brass bands: "Form Societies of Benevolence," he said; "hold meetings at least once a week to debate the questions of the day, that relate directly to us thus keeping the masses posted in what is going on." [17] Pinchback's political wisdom was absorbed and acted upon in New Orleans, and benevolent societies and sociopolitical clubs became one medium through which black street bands were born.

Pinchback's biographer mentions the frequent formation of marching clubs, quasimilitary rifle clubs, and drill teams during the hectic, often violent, Reconstruction political squabbles. One brass band is mentioned by name—Charley Jaeger's Band—as a favorite in Pinchback's processions and rallies. [18] Undoubtedly many bands formed as musical auxiliaries to political groups during these turbulent times. The bands and their descendants were those mentioned by James M. Trotter in his late-1870s survey of New Orleans music. There is no way to know how these bands sounded or what their musical practices were, but we do know that they developed early in the black community and that they were associated with the cause of black freedom and political advancement —a proud beginning for a tradition.

One link between later brass bands and the genesis of the musical style in Reconstruction politics can be traced to Magnolia plantation. A large, sugar-producing agricultural industry in Plaquemines Parish, Magnolia was founded in 1874 by Henry Clay Warmouth, the most famous (or infamous) "carpetbag" governor of Louisiana (1868–1872). [19] Warmoth, a white politician who worked with Pinchback, O. J. Dunn, and other black leaders, retired from politics to his sugar industry; and on the plantation he maintained a number of black brass bands, possibly as nostalgic mementoes of the glorious years of Reconstruction and the fight for black freedom. Warmoth hired James Humphrey to tutor his bandsmen, and many of the most famous New Orleans street musicians learned under Humphrey at Magnolia plantation. [20] It was a seedbed for the generation of brass bandsmen who would mark the genesis of jazz.

Records of another early appearance of black bands

in New Orleans are clouded by confusion. The memorial service and funeral parade for President James A. Garfield on September 27, 1881, was one of the greatest public ceremonies in the city after the Civil War. New Orleans turned out *en masse* in mourning, and thousands of marchers participated in a gigantic parade. Each marching unit included in the entourage was headed by a brass band. Music historians have asserted that a large number of black brass bands was present: "In 1881, in the funeral ceremonies for President Garfield, there was a huge procession replete with bands as usual. In this procession, some thirteen or more permanently organized Negro bands took part."[21] The idea has been repeated and distorted elsewhere: "A dozen black bands took part in the mammoth funeral cortege for President Garfield in 1881."[22] Contemporary reporting does not enumerate the bands in the parade or identify them. The New Orleans *Picayune*, in extensive and detailed coverage, lists about a dozen marching units, identifying some as black, and mentions that each group was headed by a band—but nowhere are the bands named or identified as black or white. We can assume that some were black street bands, but we cannot assume that they were permanently organized groups.

However vague our data on this period may be, we do know that the excitement and social change accompanying Reconstruction nourished the black brass-band tradition in New Orleans. The stimulus of Emancipation, the prolonged presence of Federal troops and military bands in the city, the promise of social and political equality for black people contributed to the style and content of the music. Much like the spirituals and jubilees of slavery times, this band music was born of an intense, emotionally charged desire for freedom and recognition. Its militancy is not of the battlefield or the church, but of the political arena; and it reflects the great expectations of black people in the years following their official release from bondage.

The most obscure source feeding into the New Orleans black brass-band tradition is that of self-schooled country bands. We have scant documentation of the many bands that had existed since the nineteenth century in the rural South. Frederic Ramsey, Jr., made one documentary recording of two such bands in Alabama and described them as they were in 1954.[23] Rural bands, formed by untrained musicians on isolated plantations across the South, were hardly the equivalent of schooled and polished bands in a city like New Orleans, but they represented one outlet for black musicians following the Civil War. Ramsey interviewed the bandsmen he discovered and drew some conclusions about the genesis of their groups:

The essential point to be noted, in connection with all the Negro brass bands formed shortly after Emancipation, is that they played without instruction, and picked up their tunes by ear: "Well, I tell you how it was. It was just . . . you take a fellow, he'll set down, if he hearin' 'bout a sing, a hymn . . . or hear anything like that. Well, after he got it prompt in his mind, then he'll pick up his horn. Then he'll try to play it, you see? That's the way it was. They first start playing spirituals . . . got them at the church. They go way back. . . . Sometimes us' leader . . . us' captain . . . set down and play a new piece. He'll jump out there on it. . . . Some people plays by note, and they can't jump on them notes. . . . We'll hit a piece, an' anybody can jump."

In isolated rural areas, this tradition of self-training and improvised techique was the only way a newly emancipated black man could learn music. In New Orleans, where a long tradition of freedmen and Creoles of color existed, where first-rate black musicians had been carefully trained for a century, such expedients were rare. Yet some musicians who later joined city brass bands underwent the process of self-teaching that Ramsey outlines.

The bands Ramsey recorded were crude, small ensembles, playing in only a few keys. Unacquainted with either music-reading or sophisticated instrumental techniques, they nevertheless created a coherent musical organization and a sizable repertoire drawn from their immediate environment. Their music was not a formalized genre created for wind instruments, but adaptations of the plentiful vocal music that was their only ready musical material:

The music played by members of these early plantation brass bands was based on *song*—they blew *singing horns*. Their repertoire came, not from the white man's stock of patriotic sheet music, but from church and secular songs. From the church side, they played spirituals, jubilees, and possibly, some early chants. They had probably sung them in their churches and homes before blowing them through their horns. From the everyday, or secular life, they adapted rags, reels, blues, and ballads. Later, they picked up secular tunes from "people who went through—hear a guitar fellow pickin' a guitar . . . he be pickin' reels. Us boys would catch that from it."

The practices of these rough plantation bands indicate one musical influence that was as strong in New Orleans as in the country—the powerful and exuberant vocal music of the black churches. Just as country musicians "caught" by ear spirituals and hymns, brass bands in New Orleans would play "head" arrangements of simple hymn tunes like "What a Friend We Have in Jesus" or "In the Upper Garden," or they would read rudimentary arrangements sketched from four-part vocal music in church hymnals.

Country bands also reflected, in simplified form, technical practices and stylistic traits noticeable in New Orleans bands. They used very loose polyphony, wide (vocal) vibrato, often-shaky intonation, and they concentrated on raw rhythmic energy and power. Like most "homemade" bands, the country bands produced a loud and vigorous ensemble sound, ignoring subtle dynamic shadings and intricate part-relationships. In this kind of group, as in any ensemble designed essentially for outdoor playing against much background noise, the tendency is to play always at full volume; thus the band's dynamic balance was achieved simply by every musician playing at maximum loudness. (This recalls the ubiquitous apocryphal tale about the village bandsman who explained his group's music-reading abilities by saying, "We understood *ff* to mean 'full force,' but we thought *pp* meant 'plenty powerful.'") While New Orleans brass bands worked at more sophisticated levels than the country bands and benefited from having skilled reading musicians in their ranks, they also used many of the ear-playing practices of the self-tutored country bands.

City bandsmen learned from each other and from skilled teachers. And the mixing of these carefully trained black musicians with self-taught players created ensembles that drew on both kinds of skills for repertoires and styles. The sheer number of bands also helped, through competition and trading of members, to enrich the whole musical environment.

One source of musical fashion was the traveling troupe—circuses, medicine shows, and minstrel shows, all types of nineteenth-century show business. In addition to circulating a highly conventionalized, popular (and fictitious) view of southern life, the minstrel shows gauged and shaped public taste. Extravaganzas with such splendid names as the Louisiana Slave Troupe and Brass Band (1875) or Smallwood's Great Contraband Minstrels and Brass Band (1865)[24] were familiar across the nation, and they explicitly connected black music and marching bands:

Although dominated by the plantation and religious songs, black minstrelsy also evolved other distinctive features, particularly the uniformed black marching unit, which be-

gan as just another act that black and white minstrels shared. In 1875–76 Callender's Minstrels closed the first part of their show with a "ludicrous military burlesque." Such lampoons of black soldiers had been occasional minstrel features since the Civil War, but this skit proved so popular that it became the standard finale for the first part of the black minstrel show.[25]

These shows were familiar to New Orleanians, through one of the most famous black minstrels, Billy Kersands: "One of the most widely praised acts in Kersands' Minstrels was his marching band, which led the Mardi Gras parade in 1886. Kersands even offered $1,000 to any group that could beat them in drilling and parading."[26] The example of spectacular minstrel-show acts must have prompted admiration and imitation by New Orleans' local brass bandsmen.

By the 1880s the resort/amusement area called West End (north of the city, on Lake Pontchartrain) was a platform for band music through the summer months. Concert bands from the North as well as local groups presented concerts of marches, polkas, waltzes, wind adaptations of light classics, and potpourris of popular tunes. By 1892, when Patrick Gilmore died, John Philip Sousa had left the United States Marine Band to form his own touring concert band, and Thomas Preston Brooke was organizing his Chicago Marine Band. There was a burgeoning industry for touring bands as major entertainment vehicles. West End was one resort out of dozens of similar places (Manhattan Beach, near New York City, was

An Odd Fellows parade underway, *October, 1955. Note the order of the marchers: standard bearers and marshalls, George Williams' Brass Band, uniformed club members, ladies' auxiliary. Left to right bandsmen: Edmond "Son" Washington, Joe Phillips, Theodore Riley, Steve Angrum, Ernest Poree, Bob Thomas, Bill Brown, "Buster" Moore "The Odd Fellows had funerals every day . . . music funerals, too, you know."—Isidore Barbarin, William Ransom Hogan Jazz Archive interview, January 17, 1959, pp. 36–37.*

the most celebrated) where bands set up residence to play for vacationers. Thus polished professional ensembles met large audiences in relaxed, pleasant surroundings, and America's band music became synonymous with simple, middle-class family pleasures. This was a different order of entertainment from the formal atmosphere surrounding the opera or symphonic music of the upper classes. And this distinction of class and caste was significant in the development of the brass band as an amateur avocational interest of wide popular appeal, free of snobbery or social pretension. In H. Wiley Hitchcock's useful terminology, bands became a point of fusion for both "cultivated" and "vernacular" musics.[27]

At West End in 1893, Jules Levy, the most famous (and most temperamental) of the era's great cornet virtuosi, appeared with George A. Paoletti's New Orleans ensemble—"Prof. Paoletti's Celebrated West End Band"—for a series of concerts.[28] At the turn of the century, T. P. Brooke brought his Chicago Marine Band to New Orleans for winter seasons, and in 1906 he opened his own music hall, Brooke's Winter Garden.[29] Other bands from outside the city (Herman Bellstedt's Cincinnati Band, A. Fred Weldon's Chicago group) appeared in New Orleans for regular concert programs at the resorts.[30] So the city was thoroughly exposed to the greater band movement of America.

These visiting bands did not confine themselves to warhorses in the repertoire or to polite dance music. In addition to overtures, potpourris of traditional dance tunes, and standard marches, they played popular music of immediate appeal. That meant, in the 1890s, cakewalks and "coon songs" and various imitations of these genres for wind band—patrols, plantation songs, synthetic "slave ditties." By 1900 it meant renditions of ragtime in brass. This was not, generally, anything like the classic ragtime of Scott Joplin, James Scott, Tom Turpin, Charles Hunter, and their like, the Missouri/midwestern ragtime for piano; it was, rather, an imitation of classic ragtime produced by popular songwriters and arrangers for large publishing companies. This music would dominate the popular imagination for the next fifteen years, and brass-band conductors quickly saw its audience appeal. John Philip Sousa, as conservative a bandmaster of the old school as lived, presented this popularized ragtime in his concerts beginning about 1900, and his talented trombone soloist, Arthur Pryor, made much of his reputation by arranging and conducting ragtime for band, both with Sousa and under his own name.

T. P. Brooke, who was called the "Popular Music King" by his audiences, also quickly sensed the trends in popular music, and from 1900 to 1906 he presented many concerts made up entirely of ragtime arrangements, both in New Orleans and on tour across the United States. A typical Brooke ragtime concert was presented shortly after the opening of his Winter Garden in New Orleans in 1906. The program for this concert shows that Brooke (and his audience) considered ragtime almost anything in the line of popular music, especially musical comedy numbers:[31]

Brooke Winter Garden

The large and fashionable audience that was in attendance at the Brooke Winter Garden last night thoroughly enjoyed the fine music rendered by this splendid band. This evening Mr. Brooke will play one of his famous "ragtime" concerts. In Chicago, Cincinnati, Philadelphia, Boston and other leading cities these concerts enjoyed the patronage of the society people and will doubtless prove a feature with them here. Tonight's programme in full is as follows:

The First Brooke "Ragtime" Concert.

PART FIRST.

1. A Rag March—"Peter Piper" . . . . Henry
2. Popular Rag Melodies from "Little Johnny Jones" . . . . Cohan
   Containing—Introduction, "Give My Regards to Broadway," "They're All My Friends," "Good-bye, Flo," "Nesting in a New York Tree," "If Mr. Boston Lawson Has His Way," and "Yankee Doodle Boy."
3. An African Rag—"Jungle Echoes" . . . . Hildreth
4. Choice Rags Picked Up by "The Umpire" . . . . . Howard
   Containing—"The Drums of the Fore and Aft," "Cross Your Heart," "Let's Take a Trolley," "How'd You Like to Be the Umpire," "The Sun That Shines on Dixieland," "You Look Awful Good to Father," "Clorindy Jackson" and finale to Act I.

PART SECOND.

5. Overture in Ragtime—"What the Brass Band Played" . . . . Haviland
   Introducing—"What the Brass Band Played," "I'm Going to See Birdie To-night," "Make a Fuss Over Me," "Please Come and Play in My Yard," "Longing for You," "Good-bye, Sis," "Dear Old Girl" and "A Little Boy Called Taps."

6. A Little Rag for the Piccolo—"Only Teasing" . . Arnold
   Mr. Julius Furzman
7. A Louisiana Scene—"Plantation Sounds" . . . . Dr. T. A. Duggan
8. A Ragtime Collection from "Mexicana" . . . . Hubbell
   Introducing—"I Have Heard So Much About You," "Major Margery," "The Fickle Weather Vane," "I'm the Wizard of Wall Street," "I Was Just Supposing," "We've Got a Lot to Learn" and "United We Stand."

Intermission, ten minutes.

PART THIRD.

9. Melange de Rag—"The Monarch" . . . . O'Hare
   Containing—"On the Rocky Road to Dublin," "Take Me to Your Heart Again," "When Love Is Young," "Only a Message From Home Sweet Home," "Bill Simmons," "In My Merry Oldsmobile," "Will You Love Me in December as You Do in May" and "Cupid Is the Captain of the Army."
10. A Ragtime Humoresque—"Dixie's Troubles" . . . . Wheeler
11. The Last One—"And the World Moves On" . . . . Recker

Conductor . . . . Thomas Preston Brooke

Essentially this is what we now call a pops concert, drawing on current Broadway musicals and fashionable sentimental music. However far the program was from classic ragtime, this was a step toward authentic Afro-American musical ideas. And it was evidently well received, for Brooke presented regular "all-ragtime" concerts during his New Orleans stand.

By 1911 a local band at New Orleans' City Park played this concert:[32]

Rag Time Music
City Park Program

The following programme, with moving pictures at 8 and 10 P.M., will be offered Sunday evening by the G. B. Mars concert band, at City Park:

"Rag-a-Tag Rag" . . . . Brown
"Alexander's Rag Time Band" . . . . Berlin
"Chanticleer Rag" . . . . Gumble
"Oh, That Beautiful Rag" . . . . Berlin and Snyder
"Some of These Days" . . . . Brooks
(a) "Miss Trombone" (comic trombone solo), by Mlle. S. Berendsohn
(b) "Teddy Trombone" (brother to Miss Trombone), duet by Mlle. S. Berendsohn and Monsieur William Cross.
(a) "Chicken Reel" . . . . Daly
(b) "Mr. Rooster" . . . . Lampe
(Two poultry rags)
"Italian Rag" . . . . Piantadosi
"Oh, You Drummers" (characteristic drum solo), by Ed Mars and M. Volz.
A bunch of rags (introducing "Cotton Time," "The Occana Roll," "The Georgia Rag," "A Slippery Place," "That Peculiar Rag," and "Any Rags." Arranged by G. B. Mars.
"The Empire City," a home rag . . . . Frank Broekhaven
"Down in Yucatan," characteristic rag . . . . Henry
"Grizzly Bear" . . . . Berlin and Snyder
"Dope," rag novelette . . . . Powell
That tired rag, "We're All In, Down and Out" . . Blanke

Several points are notable in this program. It is made up almost entirely of Tin Pan Alley versions of ragtime. It includes several novelty pieces for the trombone that was then in great vogue (the introduction of the slide trombone into the brass band, supplant-

ing old valved instruments, caused great popular stir, and pieces featuring endless trombone portamenti—"slurs" or "smears"—were of enduring interest; literally hundreds, like these by Cincinnati bandmaster Henry Fillmore, appeared in the first decade of the century). Several timely and important names appear: Irving Berlin is represented three times, twice with his partner Ted Snyder, at the beginning of his career as America's most enduring tunesmith; Shelton Brooks's evergreen "Some of These Days" also appears (the bands were in close touch with the "Top 40" of 1911). And, finally, the repertoire reflects activity in composing and arranging by such New Orleanians as G. B. Mars and Frank Broekhaven.

Beginning about 1900 such concerts were increasingly popular. This brought brass bands squarely into the mainstream of popular music, removing them from a specialized category of concert or holiday/ceremonial music. The repertoire for the brass band widened to encompass all popular music, especially the new music built on syncopated Afro-American rhythms. To demonstrate how bands introduced this music to New Orleans audiences in the first decade of the twentieth century, we can sample titles from band programs in the New Orleans *Item*:

JULY 1, 1900: A. F. Weldon's Second Regiment Band includes in a concert William Krell's "Levee Pastime" and Scouton's Danse Ethiopian, "Shuffling Jasper." (Krell was the bandleader-arranger who published

A campus parade at Tulane University, Derby Day, 1962. This is the revived Onward Brass Band, directed by Paul Barbarin; and it is a true brass band, using mellophone and baritone horn as the middle-range brass section. Left to right: Louis Barbarin, Paul Barbarin, Ernie Cagnolatti, Louis Cottrell, Jr., Jack Willis, Louis Nelson, Jerry Greene. "All we had in the band, as a rule, would be composed of a bass horn, one trombone, one trumpet, an alto and maybe a baritone, a clarinet, and a bass drum and a snare drum. About seven or eight pieces would be all we'd have, and brother, I'm tellin' you—talk about noise! You never heard no sixty-piece band could make as much noise as those few guys could make."—Jelly Roll Morton, Library of Congress interview (1938).

the music first copyrighted as a "rag"—"Mississippi Rag," 1897.)

MARCH 17, 1901: T. P. Brooke's Chicago Marine Band plays in concert Abe Holzmann's cakewalk-marches "Hunky Dory" and "A Bunch O' Blackberries."

JULY 5, 1903: Armand Veazey's Band plays Porter Steele's "High Society" march, a tune later famous in jazz history.

JULY 12, 1903: At West End, Veazey's Military Band plays J. Bodewalt Lampe's great hit, "Creole Belles"; at City Park, Sporer's Concert Band plays Lampe's "Dixie Girl" and "Blaze Away" and "Alagazam" by Abe Holzmann (both of these ragtime arrangers were march-writers, pointing up the basic connections between ragtime and the standard march form); at Audubon Park, William J. Braun's Naval Brigade Band includes in its program Cole and Johnson's "Under the Bamboo Tree" and two of the newest classic rags from Missouri, Tom Turpin's "The Bowery Buck" and "A Ragtime Nightmare."

JULY 26, 1903: Armand Veazey's Band plays "Hiawatha" by "Neil Moret" (Charles N. Daniel), the ragtime tune that introduced the "Indian Intermezzo" vogue, a number still played by jazz bands, often under a parody title, "Lizard on a Rail."

AUGUST 2, 1903: Braun's Naval Brigade Band plays "Southern Smiles" and "Peaceful Henry," by E. H. Kelly, two typical Kansas City rags.

FEBRUARY 7, 1904: Boehler's First Regiment Band plays J. Bodewalt Lampe's "Dixie Girl" and Kelly's "Peaceful Henry"; the influence of successful commercial ragtime arrangers is here evident.

This roster demonstrates that New Orleans' concert bands playing for large popular audiences acknowledged the latest vogue in commercial music publishing and catered to a demand for syncopated hits.

Thus a general public developed for ragtime music —meaning here, popular songs and arranged commercial adaptations of piano ragtime. Simultaneously, another early tradition of "ragtime" developed—performance of *improvised* syncopated music by small brass bands, what older musicians called "head music" or "ratty" playing. This tradition is separate from the formal military-style brass bands, the polished concert bands of West End—separate, but not disconnected. Bandsmen in small black brass bands inhabited the musical landscape from which the other groups grew. They borrowed tunes like "High Society" or "My Maryland" from the repertoire of music-reading bands. They learned standard marches like "Our Director" or "National Emblem." They patterned themselves on the brass band as it was generally known, using as far as they could the same instruments and instrumental balance.

In the 1880s several permanently organized black brass bands had formed—the Excelsior Brass Band and the Onward Brass Band. From this time on, more small bands sprang up, some enduring as permanent units for many years, others quickly disbanding. The typical pattern for forming and maintaining these bands is described by Charles Love, whose father was of this generation: "My father had a band. At that time there the fellows used to have a meetin'; everytime they had a meetin' they'd put so much money up until they get enough, and they'd buy a set of instruments. And they would rehearsal together, they had a teacher and when they sent and got those instruments, they had the understandin' that any fellow would quit the band he had to leave his instrument, if he was gonna quit and go away, or something like that. He'd leave, he'd leave his instrument with the band."[33] The bands formed as clubs of amateur musicians and organized to buy the instruments, uniforms, and music necessary. The next step was to find a teacher to coordinate untrained players and work with them in an ensemble (and individually) until the group could play its music.

Charles "Sunny" Henry described James Humphrey's instruction of his thirteen-piece Eclipse Brass Band, which played occasionally in the city:

The first way he'd do, he would get the band on its foots, you see, and then he'd commence with his trumpet, and then, again, he'd get 'em all straight first, you see. But the first thing he would do, that battery [Fr., *battre*, drum]—that's the first thing he would get straight first, that battery . . . that's the bass and the trombone and the drum and everything—after he'd get all that straight first, and then he'd jump on the trumpets, you see, and he'd get them. Because that battery, that's the foundation of the band, you see. And so when he'd get that straight, then after that, the trumpets, you see—he'd get on them. And then, when he'd get them straight, all right, he'd say, "Come on, let's go; everybody." But what he would do, he would make that battery get in there first, you understand, and get everybody straight first, and then, trumpets. I gone tell you, the way he taught the boys, I think it was the right way.[34]

This is a rudimentary training program for ensemble —working through a new piece of music, starting with rhythm/bass elements (the point of genesis in Afro-American music), and going on to lead/melodic elements. Henry describes Humphrey working with the band twice a week for three or four hours at a time —a demanding rehearsal schedule for an amateur band! The band was made up of four cornets, two clarinets, two alto horns, one baritone horn, one trombone, one tuba, and bass and snare drums.[35] This is close to the pattern of early black street bands of New Orleans, with a little more emphasis on cornets, clarinets, and alto horns and less emphasis on trombones.

James Humphrey also wrote scores for the band— marches and other exercises. William "Baba" Ridgley mentions that Humphrey came into the city to coach a brass band Ridgley had formed at about the same time. According to Ridgley, Humphrey wrote arrangements of marches, songs, and hymns already familiar to the bandsmen. He then rehearsed the men through the tunes, emphasizing music-reading skills and in-

A Masonic parade, *summer, 1952, with the Eureka Brass Band. Note the white summer uniforms and the Masonic aprons on lodge members. Left to right: Albert Warner, "Sunny" Henry, Emanuel Paul, Percy Humphrey, Joseph "Red" Clark, "Kid Shiek" Colar, Ruben Roddy, Robert Lewis, Willie Pajaud.*

strumental techniques. This in about 1895, with a twelve-piece brass band! Ridgley greatly admired Humphrey's skill and insights into the musicians' problems.[36]

According to older brass bandsmen like Henry and Ridgley, bands of this period were strict "reading" bands, playing from scores, without faking or head music. Teachers like Humphrey concentrated on teaching the musicians to read different music—waltzes, marches in the cavalry mode (6/8 meter), and other forms, as well as standard "split" time (2/4) marches. Henry emphasized the necessity for careful reading in the older bands: "When you get in there—let me tell you: in that Excelsior Band and Onward Band and Tuxedo Band—well, I'll tell you—and Allen Band, too—you know, then, you just had to know your stuff, or else know—you got to have a mighty good head to play in that band if you couldn't read. Course, if you could read some, well, you could make out, you understand. But them people, you used to put them old heavy marches on you, you had to jump."[37] The older musicians referred to march scores as "heavy" music—*i.e.*, complex scores with densely written ("black") parts requiring concentration in reading. Black brass bands of the 1880s and 1890s cut their teeth on this material.[38] With this repertoire the Excelsior Brass Band, the Eclipse Brass Band from Magnolia plantation, and the Onward Brass Band played concerts, dances, or parades.

Many of the marches played by New Orleans brass bands were read—or adapted—from stock band scores distributed by popular publishers like Henry Fillmore's Cincinnati company. At the turn of the century a large quantity of new marches and other band scores was available. As with such favorite street marches as "High Society" and "Panama," adapted from popular music hits, other New Orleans marches derive from written sources, orthodox military-band arrangements. Examples are "Salutation March," written and published by Roland A. Seitz in 1916; "Gettysburg March," written by S. B. Stambaugh and published by Fillmore in 1911. And for the tune called "Bugle Boy March" in New Orleans, there are two possible sources—"American Soldier March," written and published by A. S. Josselyn in 1904, or "American Soldier March and Two-Step," written by Francis A. Myers and published by Fillmore in 1907. These marches were transmitted by tradition and altered by improvisational techniques, but they were originally created in the standard march idiom.

We can assume that top band musicians were skilled readers and that their usual repertoire was comprised of the era's standard band music, including marches, popular dance tunes, light classics. Only at the turn of the century, as the music we now call jazz began to be amalgamated by nonreading musicians, did brass bands incorporate much head music into their repertoires. Only slowly did they shift from reading standard printed band arrangements to developing improvisational, head arrangements.

Peter Bocage, who played with brass bands from the Excelsior Brass Band in the 1920s through the Eureka Brass Band in the 1960s, described the impact of improvisational music at the turn of the century:

Well, I attribute it to [Charles "Buddy"] Bolden, you know; I mean, cause—the simple fact, the way that thing came about—you see, Bolden was a fellow, he didn't know a note as big as this house, you understand what I mean; and whatever they played, they caught [learned by ear] or made up, you see? Say—they made their own music, and they played it their own way, you understand? So that's the way jazz started, you understand?—just through the feeling of the man, you understand?—his, his improvisation, you see. . . . But the old time musicians, they didn't play nothing but music, you know.[39]

Bocage distinguished between reading musicians ("nothing but music") and "routine" musicians—i.e., musicians who learned head arrangements by listening to the band and memorizing ("catching"). He felt these musicians, unlike those trained in reading, led to jazz practices in brass-band playing: "Now, you take a lot of those fellows, they were routine players, and that's where jazz came from, ya understand. . . . They just made up their own ideas. They didn't know nothin' about phrasing, nothing in music—no thoughts at all about music. Just go ahead and play, that's all, ya understand. That's how jazz came about."[40] The tension between the reading musician and the "ear" musician surfaces in Bocage's remarks; when he uses the word *music*, he refers to *written* scores, musical nota-

tion. Clearly Bocage preferred the older methods of the reading bands, though he worked with brass bands throughout his career—primarily because the bands continued to rely on some reading, especially for difficult dirge parts in funeral processions. Thus there was always a place for a trained brass musician like Bocage or Manuel Perez or Willie Pajaud, trumpet men specializing in lyrical dirge solos.

Bocage, through half a century's experience with brass bands, saw the changes in the tradition, the shift from strict reading bands to improvising jazz bands: "When I was a little boy they had the Excelsiors, and they had what they called the Old Onward Band—now that was all old-time musicians, all—nothing strictly but marches, you understand; no jazz, no none of that. When they played, they played nothing but those marches, see."[41] Bocage joined the Excelsior Brass Band and inherited its leadership from George Moret. At this time—in the early 1920s—the repertoire widened:

We played a lot of marches, too, and we used to mix up a little jazz in there, see? But now the brass bands of today, practically most—it seems like the public wants it, and that's what they're giving them is mostly all jazz, you see? —outside of funeral marches, you know. . . . But years ago it was different, you know—the people wanted marches, and nice, and the band sounds so much nicer when you're playing good, standard music. . . . And you take a good say ten or twelve piece brass band, and everybody playing their parts; it's wonderful.[42]

Peter Bocage was born in 1887; he grew up with the shift from the earliest reading bands and the rise of the new dance music called jazz. It was around the time of Bocage's birth that the Excelsior Brass Band and the Onward Brass Band were established as "legitimate" reading bands presenting concerts and marching in parades. As early as 1881 the Excelsior Brass Band was available for holiday parades, as reflected in the New Orleans *Picayune*, August 15, 1881: "The Pickwick Base Ball Club gave the pic-nic, which was attended by nearly two thousand persons. This club, Mr. W. H. Cohen, captain, paraded through the principal streets of the city in the morning, preceded by the Excelsior Brass Band of sixteen pieces." By the 1890s these bands gave concerts for the black population, imitating fashionable concerts at West End. The Onward Brass Band played at Spanish Fort, a resort/amusement area eastward down the shore of Lake Pontchartrain from West End:

Beautiful Resort for the Colored People

At Spanish Fort next Sunday a musical concert will be given in the park from 2:30 until 6:00 P.M. by the Onward Brass Band.

These concerts are free and are being liberally attended by the best families of the colored people of our city.

Spanish Fort is not only an historic place, but a beautiful one.

These concerts are given from the band stand, located in the center of the park. Numerous settees are scattered about the stand and throughout the grounds underneath the trees, for the comfort of visitors.[43]

At the same time, black brass bands appeared in various ceremonial functions connected with social clubs: "The Chalmette Benevolent Association of the lower districts on Thursday last installed the officers elected for the ensuing year 1890. After the ceremonies the association, headed by the Eagle Brass Band, proceeded to the residence of the grand marshal, A. Burche, and partook of refreshments. They then serenaded their officers and friends."[44]

Another newspaper item demonstrates that street parades in New Orleans, even then, could be dangerous. The article chronicles a clash between exuberant "second liners" and other bystanders, a tradition of impromptu violence also mentioned by Jelly Roll Morton[45] and others as a risk inherent in parading:

Brickbatting a Negro Procession. Young White Hoodlums Bring on a Riot in Which Several Persons are Injured.

About 3:30 o'clock Sunday afternoon in the fourth district a small-sized riot took place between a crowd of negroes and whites, during which rocks, bricks and clubs were freely used and several persons were slightly injured.

It appears that a colored procession headed by the Onward Brass Band was marching out Washington street. They intended serenading a colored woman, Mrs. Johnson, mother of one of the members. The usual crowd of negroes who follow parades of this kind were on hand in force and took charge of the sidewalk as is their custom.

The procession reached the corner of Magazine and Washington . . . when the negroes on the sidewalk were attacked by a force of young white men, who pelted them with rocks, etc. This was a signal for a general battle on all sides. The entire neighborhood turned out and men, women and chil-

Photo courtesy F. Jack Hurley

The very model of a grand marshall:
Matthew "Fats" Houston, with the Eureka Brass Band in the French Quarter, summer, 1962. Oscar "Chicken" Henry peers over the magisterial shoulder.

dren were seen running from all directions to escape the flying rocks and brickbats.

The greatest excitement prevailed and several people made their appearance armed with shotguns.

The paraders and members of the band also took a hand in the row, which lasted until reaching the corner of Magazine and Washington streets.[46]

Most of the traditions brass bands followed later were established before the turn of the century. At least two well-organized bands—Excelsior and Onward—played concerts and parades regularly. During the late 1880s the bands most often mentioned in the newspapers were the Onward, the Alliance, the Pickwick and, above all, the Excelsior. The last group earned a reputation for reliability and appeared in varied settings. Columns of the *Weekly Pelican*, a black-edited New Orleans newspaper supporting Republican efforts during the post-Reconstruction era, repeatedly cited the Excelsior band from 1887 to 1889. The *Pelican* files record the uses of brass bands; nearly every week bands are reported at social club or fraternal order meetings, at church dances and festivals, at private parties and street parades. Also recorded in these columns are the names of early band personnel:

The Crescent City band, with J. P. Monroe as manager and W. M. Jackson as leader, furnished excellent music. (March 14, 1887)

The Gayten brass band has been organized. Mr. C. H. Gayten is manager.

The Onward brass band, under the leadership of Prof. J. O. Lainez, have received their new caps. A torch is attached to the caps. (September 10, 1887)

The PELICAN Brass Band was organized on the 23rd of January, 1889, with Mr. J. Dresch as leader and Messrs. S. S. Decker, J. B. Humphrey, E. J. Palao, J. O. Hoggat, J. T. Hall, Samuel Kincey, William Crawford, A. W. Clark, J. T. Bates, Jas. Bernard, Jas. Taylor as members. (March 2, 1889)

The Alliance brass band is composed of some our most intelligent colored citizens and will before long make a well-earned reputation. Mr. F. J. Clermont is the general manager and Mr. E. J. Duplessis and Henry Black agents for the band. (April 20, 1889)

We find out a few months later (October 26, 1889) that the Alliance Brass Band was led by Victor Lacorbiere.[47] We also find out a little about the early leadership of the Excelsior Brass Band: "The Ladies' Vidalia Benevolent Association gave their first grand fancy dress and calico ball . . . [with] the famous Excelsior Brass Band, under the leadership of Prof. Baqué, to play for the occasion" (October 19, 1889). This is Theogene Baquet, E^b clarinetist, who led the Excelsior before George Moret took it over. The columns of this newspaper also report on activities of music teachers instrumental in organizing and coaching bands of this and the next generation—men like William Nickerson and James Humphrey. In 1887, while Nickerson was on tour with a musical road show company, Humphrey took his position as director of the Straight and Southern University bands and orchestras. Black musicians of this period were interconnected through string bands and small orchestras that employed musicians doubling on instruments (mentioned are ensembles such as the Onward String Band and the Excelsior String Orchestra).

The most successful and lauded Excelsior Brass Band had a reputation beyond New Orleans. In 1887 the bandsmen left the city for a protracted tour, and the March 30, 1887, issue of the *Pelican* reported:

The Excelsior brass band of this city, will leave the city about the middle of May for a six month tour through the North and East, having been engaged by a prominent manager who heard of their excellent musical ability. His [*sic*] manager will be here to-morrow to close the contract. They will have new uniforms made for sixteen men. They will visit Baltimore, Philadelphia, New York, Boston and other cities. The boys certainly ought to feel proud of this as a compliment to them of no mean order. Good wishes of their many friends go with them.

These brief and vague newspaper squibs give glimpses of the bands in their milieu. We know a sixteen-piece band was standard (as for most small-town groups of the era), that band musicians worked in dance orchestras and other aggregations, that brass bands played for dancing and for formal parties, as well as on the streets or for lawn parties and picnics. From this we can deduce something about the broadness and flexibility of their repertoires and styles.

We glimpse the gaiety of celebrations in which bands played: "The Larendon Rifles, headed by the Onward Brass Band, had a royal time new year's eve. They paraded the principal streets and serenaded Messrs. Geo. Q. Whitney, Geo. A. Trauth, Herbert Finch and A. H. Edmunds, after which they proceeded to the residence of Mr. Henry Banks, on Philip Street, where they were entertained at supper" (January 8, 1887). The scene must have been vivid—bright uniforms of band and drill team, brass buttons, gold-braid epaulets and frogs, peaked caps, torchlight and gaslight flashing on nickel plating of cornets and horns, a procession of exuberant followers in the van and wake of the band, laughter, bright notes in crisp dark air. A brief notation of another gala event cites a brilliant occasion for the musicians: "There were ten colored bands in the Fireman's parade on the 4th of March. Three of them were from adjacent towns" (March 12, 1887). An earlier entry in the *Weekly Pelican* had mentioned further details: "Two of Thibodaux's crack colored bands came down to participate in the fireman's parade—the Excelsior and Eureka bands" (March 5, 1887). So we learn that the grand names common to New Orleans brass bands were in use elsewhere.[48] This upstate town supplied two black units bearing names famous in the history of New Orleans brass musicians. The parade itself must have provided a grand occasion—the uniforms and brightwork of the fire companies competing with the equally brilliant costumes and instruments of ten brass bands in procession. And over all there reigned the sound of martial music.

The main impression such snatches of early reporting give is that bands were profuse and active. We have ample evidence of the healthy state of the art of brass bandsmanship in the 1880s, the decade before the emergence of ragtime on the streets. The success of these bands led to organization of more bands and a tradition of black band music on public occasions.

Two other ceremonial occasions for brass band are documented in news files of 1890. Although neither item refers to black groups, both indicate the uses of bands before the advent of ragtime. The first item describes a cornerstone laying, a ceremony regularly attended by a brass band, as a component of the Masonic ritual for the dedication:

Mr. John A. Morris, who has dotted our town [Washington, Louisiana] with a cotton factory, has tendered a most gracious invitation to the Corona Band to attend the laying of the cornerstone of the Caffrey central sugar refinery in St. Mary parish, which event will take place Monday next, the 28th inst. Mr. Morris pays all the expenses, railroad fare and hotel bills, etc. The board of directors and several prominent Washingtonians were also invited. The Corona Band, which has a large membership of twenty-five tooters, have accepted the invitation, and will take the train next Monday for Franklin.[49]

This reference to a typical provincial band indicates that musicians and audience expected a local band to be prepared for such ceremonial occasions.

The second item from 1890 records a New Orleans funeral with brass band music. Even though this may have been an exceptional occasion—the death of a musician, not an average citizen—it shows that brass bands were prepared to play in funeral processions: "The funeral of Charles Peetz, one of the oldest German musicians, who died on Thursday of heart failure, took place yesterday amidst a large concourse of friends. Prof. Wolf's Military Band, assisted by members of other bands, performed the funeral dirges."[50] This continues a very old tradition of funeral processions with music and is prototypical of the funerals later closely associated with brass-band jazz. Wolf's Military Band was a concert group playing regularly at West End, and their appearance for a funeral procession, their augmentation with other bandsmen, and their playing of dirges indicates that such an ensemble was ready for the occasion. If not a main function of a municipal band, at least it was an event to which they were accustomed.

In the years before 1900 a solid tradition of both self-trained provincial bands and municipal bands of skilled musicians was firmly established in the rich musical milieu around New Orleans. These musicians would become dance band players and would participate in the creation of the characteristic syncopated dance music first called ragtime or ratty, low-down music and then generally known as jazz. The two decades 1890–1910 saw this development, in which both old-time musicians and younger men partici-

Photo courtesy F. Jack Hurley

A cornerstone-laying parade, *with the E. Gibson Brass Band, September 6, 1964. Lodge members and ladies' auxiliary follow the band, bearing the cornerstone to the church for installation ceremonies. Left to right: Carroll Blunt, A. B. Spears, Eddie Richardson, Earl Harden, George Sterling, Eddie Morris, Dave Bailey, Robert Davis, John Wimberly.* "In them days and time, we had to guess, we never had the teachers that they got today. Now, today's a day you can get a teacher every minute in the day. You've got teachers to learn you, but we just had to pick it up from the man above. God Almighty give a gift." — *Louis Keppard (tuba player with the E. Gibson Brass Band), William Ransom Hogan Jazz Archive interview, January 19, 1961, pp. 11–12.*

pated. Sometimes this transition or cross-fertilization between brass bands and dance bands is clear. John Robichaux, who would become perhaps the most successful and the most enduring of the city's black dance-orchestra leaders, belonged to the Excelsior Brass Band. From among its musicians he formed a formal, "sit-down" or "society" orchestra in about 1893. Robichaux's orchestra became the number-one black formal orchestra of New Orleans, playing in the best locations until 1939. Similarly, Manuel Perez, the almost-legendary trumpet player, worked with the Onward Brass Band from 1900 to 1930, while he also led one of the city's most popular and successful dance-jazz orchestras. Perez preferred to play written music with the Onward; like Peter Bocage he looked on brass-band work as a test of reading skill and technical execution, and he was famous for his solo playing in funeral dirges.

Later, most brass bandsmen would work also as dance band or jazz musicians, and brass-band work would be only an incidental part of their careers. But in the nineteenth century, the brass band served as the training ground for many black musicians, and many of these men preferred parade work to any other. Men like Sunny Henry and Albert Warner, the Eureka Brass Band's trombone team in the 1940s and 1950s, were almost exclusively brass-band musicians. Other musicians, like drummer Louis Cottrell, Sr., or like the Lorenzo Tios, father and son clarinetists renowned as the city's finest reed teachers, worked with brass bands and reading orchestras and played relatively little jazz. The tradition, as testimony from Bocage and many others shows, was one of careful reading and execution, playing "legitimate" brass-band music, until somewhere around the turn of the century when ragtime brass bands began to appear. Then "ear" musicians, "routiners" who made up head arrangements of simple tunes, began to dominate black brass bands of New Orleans.

Older musicians associated with the brass bands assert that early bands did not play ragtime. Avery "Kid" Howard, veteran of brass bands from the 1920s through the 1950s (including the Eureka Brass Band, the Pacific Brass Band, and his own units), stated that the brass bands of Manuel Perez's day—i.e., from the turn of the century through the 1920s—played straight marches and other scored music. He could not recall a "tonk" brass band of the era (a group using head practices and basically playing jazz). When pressed, Kid Howard said that Chris Kelly and Henry "Kid" Rena sometimes organized very rough "jump-up" (pick-up) bands like those of later decades. Howard went on to describe the bands' playing at funerals and using jazz on the way back from burials, saying that the bands would "put 'em in the alley" on the way home—i.e., play in a rough, low-down style the music especially associated with Chris Kelly, a cornetist most famous as a blues player.[51]

The nineteenth-century tradition of the strict reading bands lingered long and died hard. Peter Bocage is typical of musicians who grew up in the brass-band tradition—conservative, interested basically in reading music and using carefully scored pieces, disdainful of jazz practices that infiltrated the brass-band style. He recalled that the Excelsior Brass Band under his leadership played almost entirely "heavy" marches and gave as an example a funeral march arranged from the sextet from *Lucia*. As he recalled, everyone in the Excelsior Band read music, and they played almost entirely stock band arrangements adapted for small ensemble.[52]

Many musicians active through the 1950s were on Perez' side of the brass-band tradition—committed to trained, rehearsed bands reading stock sheet music in the most "legitimate" manner. Joseph "Red" Clark, long-time trombonist, bassist, and manager with the Eureka Brass Band, for example, was (like Bocage) an avid collector of stock arrangements for band, especially funeral marches. And Clark believed that a brass band should stick to this music. Sunny Henry, as his testimony has shown, was most interested in reading scores. Willie Pajaud, the trumpeter who specialized in dirge solos for the Eureka Brass Band, was a counterpart of Manuel Perez. The brass bands trained many great jazzmen—King Oliver, Bunk Johnson, Kid Ory, Johnny Dodds, Louis Armstrong, down an endless roster—but the men who persisted with the brass bands maintained the tradition after 1920 and did not regard themselves primarily as jazz musicians. They considered themselves "heavy" music readers, "musicians," as opposed to "ear" men and "routiners" of the nonreading jazz bands.

Across another social barrier in the city, white musicians had a different perception of the brass bands and their functions. Jack "Papa" Laine, patriarch of white New Orleans jazz, worked amidst the brass-band tradition. In the 1890s Laine began a career as a band manager and entrepreneur, organizing a series of brass bands available for hire and serving as their agent. He worked with these musicians until he retired from music at the end of World War I, and the list of distinguished white New Orleans jazzmen tutored by Laine includes virtually the whole first generation of jazz. Laine's small brass bands were hired for parades, circuses, tent shows, political rallies, parties, dances, the gamut of musical styles of the day.

Laine, interviewed in his late eighties, recalled the outline of his career, if not many specific details. In his memory, white brass bands dominated the musical scene of 1885 to 1900: "White brass bands. I remember one, one colored band, I remember that but all white brass bands, they had Professor Braun, and Broekhaven and people like that. . . . They used to play funeral marches and stuff like that too, and I got so I got in that line, too, playin' funerals, and I played many of 'em, I'm tellin' you that."[53] Laine recalled here the large concert bands of West End more than the small street bands, but he linked himself with this white tradition more clearly than with black brass bands. Later he asserted that these white bands (*i.e.*, formal concert bands), when playing funerals, played "straight" military marches, reading from scores, even returning from the funerals. He said that black bands also followed this practice.[54] He was recalling the years before "ratty" music was played after the obsequies. Laine described the process of arranging a typical march for a funeral procession:

Now stuff that we used to play, the likes of "Marching Along" and stuff like that, marches like that, was nothing—no trios much in it, see, all loud stuff, but we got along this man [Achille] Baquet and this [Dave] Perkins I'm telling you about, he arranged it so that we first, first chorus, first chorus he'd play it in the piano pitch before, you understand, then put it on heavy in the second, see, but we used to play that loud music all along till we got those fellas in there, see, to show us. Because they were old heads in music, they read music.[55]

Laine outlined an interesting process of teaching and organizing here, similar to Sunny Henry's reminiscences of James Humphrey rehearsing the Eclipse Brass Band on Magnolia plantation. There is a transition from untrained "ear" playing to rough "routine" or head arrangements derived from stock march scores. As Laine was very assertive about the beginnings of his band ("When we started to playin' it was not nothin' but ear, all ear music. Nothing else but."[56]), we can assume that the Laine aggregations were on an "earn-as-you-learn" basis, scrabbling to pick up musical sophistication and techniques as they worked together.

The other significant point about this description of Laine's bands at work is that the two teachers, Achille Baquet and Dave Perkins, were widely known as teachers and instrumentalists; both were black, and Baquet was closely associated with the black brass-band movement. His father, Theogene Baquet, led the Excelsior Brass Band, the best black group of the era, and Achille's brother George became one of the great New Orleans jazz clarinetists. Laine's men got excellent tutoring. Perkins was a brass player and drummer who taught many of the next generation of jazzmen, black and white. However crude the materials, Baquet and Perkins worked with Laine's groups to impose order on their "ear" playing and taught many musicians to read music.

Throughout his testimony, however, Laine insisted that many of the bands he organized (known under the *omnium gatherum* title "Reliance Brass Band") played improvised, "ear" music, not straight or "heavy" marches and scored arrangements. A strain of white chauvinism, mixed with self-aggrandizement, runs through Laine's talk. He tried to establish the primacy of his own work and musicians over predecessors and generally ignored black groups of his era.

This is offset by interviews with Johnny Lala, one of Laine's most apt pupils and a first-rate jazz trumpeter through the 1920s. Lala is much freer with praise for black musicians:

I remember the colored bands they had all around the city of New Orleans. There was the Imperial band, the Superior band, the Olympia, the Magnolia, Tuxedo band. All colored fellows. They go 'round—in them days they'd give a dance, and everything, the band that would play for the dance would go 'round on a truck, call it a furniture wagon. . . . And they would put sides there, you know, with a sign where the dance would be that night. In fact the white bands used to do the same thing. Jack Laine used to have three bands called the Reliance band: #1, #2, #3. And that's why how all that stuff was originated—from the Negroes.[57]

Lala here describes dance orchestras rather than street bands, but the import is clear; he credits black musicians of the era with the creative innovations. As Lala recalled his apprenticeship (he was born in 1893 and joined Laine's groups around 1910), the black street bands then played ragtime, unlike the straight white bands: "Well, the white bands was mostly military, but the colored bands, no, all popular. . . . They'd get in a parade, man, and I'm telling you. . . . Oh, man, them fellers was sitting down to go up and down St. Charles Street and Canal Street playing them military marches, we'd come along and play that hot stuff, man . . . it was something new to see a jazz band marchin'."[58] By the time Lala describes, much ragtime was on the streets.

Another early white musician, Arthur "Monk" Hazel, remembered connections with white brass bands: "My father was a bass drummer in one of the early jazz bands of New Orleans; it was called Fischer's Ragtime Military Jazz Band, and my first teacher was [Joseph] "Ragbaby" Stevens [a Laine musician], and my first job was in a Carnival parade."[59] Hazel insisted that the term *jazz* was in use before 1910 and applied to street bands like those of Laine playing "ear" music. After the turn of the century black and white bands alike played various versions of improvised ragtime music mixed with their usual repertoires of written marches, dance tunes, and ceremonial music.

At the beginning of this century, the tradition of black brass bands in New Orleans was rich, including concert music available for band, standard band marches, diverse dance music, and a whole new strain of improvised folk music nurtured in the city and unique in its complexity. Up the river in Memphis, W. C. Handy began a career as a concert bandmaster and cornetist, which in many ways parallels that of Manuel Perez in New Orleans. Handy discovered and wrote down the trove of music from Delta blues songsters, and his band played this music in concerts. In Missouri, Scott Joplin served briefly as arranger and cornetist with the Queen City Concert Band, discovering new vistas for his ragtime concepts. Joplin composed marches during his career (*e.g.*, "Cleopha" and the 6/8 marches, "Rosebud March" and "March Majestic"), and his finest rags are shaped by the march feeling—see especially "Peacherine Rag," "The Strenuous Life," or "The Favorite." In New Orleans the same process of discovery and adaptation occurred, though few local musicians bothered to document it. Rough

A Labor Day parade, *Algiers, Louisiana, 1957, with the Young Tuxedo Brass Band. Note flags and attendant benevolent association marchers. Left to right: Rudolph Beaulieu, Vernon Gilbert, John Handy, John Casimir, Eddie Pierson, Wilbert Tillman, Jim Robinson.*

nonreading musicians like Buddy Bolden mined this new strain of syncopated Afro-American folk music for their dances, and soon street bands adapted these materials. Within a few years black brass bands were playing jazz on the streets, mixed with marches and funeral music. Increasingly brass-band musicians were expected to improvise.

The generation of musicians born around 1900 grew up with this new idea and accepted it intuitively. Sunny Henry described young Louis Armstrong's apprenticeship with the street bands: "I didn't never understand Louis Armstrong, because that son-of-a-gun, he . . . didn't care what you played. . . . He would play a obbligato all the time; be off [the melody], you understand; he wouldn't never come play straight with you. But everything he put it in there, by Ned, it worked."[60] This new music, and the new men who played it, would go all around the world. The older musicians who had prepared the way would never completely accept or understand this "ragtime," this "jazz," but it was a language stronger and richer than the dialects from which it was coined.

Chapter II Walk Through the Streets of the City

When a fellow Is playing with a Red Hot Brass Band And they have all the work he dont have time to be bothered with writing no letters. . . . The boys give me H . . . all the Time because forever talking about the Brass Band and how I youster like to make those Parades. They say I dont see how A man can Be crazy about those hard Parades. I told them they dont go hard with you when you are playing with a good Band.

—Louis Armstrong to Isidore Barbarin
September 1, 1922

IF THE NEW MUSIC called jazz influenced New Orleans brass bands, reciprocal effects were equally important. The brass bands were a main influence on instrumental ragtime, not only because the musicians were veterans, however briefly, of brass-band playing, but because teachers were band-oriented and because a generation's traditions of instrumental technique had focused on the brass ensemble. Certainly, other musical traditions in the city were powerful—the French Opera and its vocal-orchestral music, string ensembles of many sizes and shapes, many varieties of folk and church singing; but the most popular instrumental model must have been the "splendid brass band" mentioned in newspaper accounts of festivities. Brass bands were everywhere, and they played the most popular airs. The sound of brass instruments was as all-pervasive as the summer heat: "There is a real mania in this city for horn and trumpet playing. You can hardly turn a corner that you do not hear some amateur attempting, in perfect agony, to perform his devotion to the God of Music. A wag remarked to us yesterday that he never before thought to have run from a *horn*, and declared, without apparent irreverence, that he earnestly desired to hear the *last* trumpet."[1] This as early as 1838! By the end of the century, New Orleans was a Babel of brass.

A significant influence from the brass bands was the difficult to describe combination of outdoor playing, with its effect on pitch and tone qualities, and the use of march polyphony. Since the aim of brass players was volume and carrying power, as noted earlier, the whole band would play at full volume and balance itself at *ff*. This taxed players' intonation and instrumental attack. Trumpet and trombone tone became hoarse and shrill. The clarinet often used on the street was the E♭ instrument, a soprano model that was coarser and shriller in tone than the usual B♭ clarinet (and also more difficult to play in tune). Ensemble sound, then, was blaring and harsh, with high clarinet and trumpet parts piercing a dense texture of middle-range sounds. The march polyphonic style added to the already-unique ensemble sound. Every player had a separate part related to other figures played, usually in the fashion of the military march—with trumpets playing a straightforward melodic lead, clarinet playing a closely related counterlead, alto and baritone horns playing rhythmic accents (an oom-pah or "peckhorn" off-beat part) or countermelody harmony parts, trombones harmonizing a counterpart, and drums and tuba holding down a strict 2/4 rhythm. This contrapuntal playing is relatively simple when a musician is following a scored arrangement, but improvising in this fashion is complex.

What happened in freer head playing was a very loose polyphonic arrangement, with some melodic lines colliding and some countermelodies remaining incomplete. To an extent this was "every tub on its own bottom," every man for himself, with the lead melody passed loosely around the band. The habit in trumpet playing was to use three trumpets, two playing a constant melodic lead and the third a second-cornet harmony. This meant one "solo" lead trumpet could rest occasionally to preserve his lip:

You have two solo men; well, one of those men got to be up [playing] all the time, see? For instance: if you was playing solo with me—like I start the band off, I'm the leader, all right. Well, I play down that—you play right along, but you rest a little while I'm playing, see; and when I get ready to rest, you come up, see, and give me a chance to rest, see? But the first man, he plays all the time, see; but he's playing the first part—it's much easier than the solo part, see? But the two solo men got to work at intervals, you see, to give each other a chance to rest.[2]

Such practices developed as self-preservation in the long parades (sometimes lasting eight hours) common in New Orleans. Other bandsmen besides the trumpet players could rest momentarily without disrupting the loose polyphony. But this gave ensembles a ragged or sporadic flow, with instruments coming in and dropping out of passages unexpectedly. A loose partnership developed between trombonists, for example, so that a pair of instruments could function as a team, playing harmonized parts or playing individually. Alto and baritone horns, or alto and tenor saxophones, would also work sometimes as a small "section" inside the ensemble. Only drums and bass were forced to play continuously.

This ensemble style paralleled practices in scored marches but was idiosyncratic enough to sound markedly different. At first the loose polyphony and variations interjected into a number might sound simply chaotic or inaccurate to a listener expecting the read-from-score, note-for-note precision of a military marching band, but careful listening shows distinct patterns in the ensemble style.

Picou's [E♭ clarinet] part could always be heard above band, usually he played rather staccato, & alternated between a couple notes & also repeated notes, somewhat in the Tesch [Frank Teschemacher] style.
    The cornets played somewhat in harmony, but frequently they would cut loose in soloistic style. . . .
    The two trombones . . . stuck pretty close together, apparently at times trying to play in unison. Even when they didn't, rhythmically they usually played similar parts. In general it was the traditional (Sousa) brass band style of counter figures, mixed in with bass parts.
    The drums did nothing fancy but were very good & were wonderfully solid together. The bass drummer, with drum strapped around "neck" played the cym[bal] also with a wire beater in left hand.[3]

This rough ensemble style, created over fifty years' playing, demanded ingenuity and creativity. Unique patterns of instrumental style thus developed, especially in terms of harmonic patterns and intonation.

The black New Orleans brass band nurtured a characteristic outdoor-playing sytle that utilized a hoarse and "crying" tone, wide vibrato, and a peculiar instrumental attack not heard in jazz and dance bands. This is easily heard but hard to describe. There is a tendency for different instrumental parts to clash with some dissonance, and the looser instrumental attack causes parts to be momentarily out of tune and time with each other. Sometimes this may be inaccuracy or ineptitude, but it is not just "sloppy" playing or musical illiteracy, as some critics charge.

New Orleans musicians *habitually adopt a characteristic "brass-band" style when they play this music.* This theory can be demonstrated by comparing the playing of George Lewis' band in its normal make-up and repertoire with the same musicians in the Original Zenith Brass Band recordings. An even better comparison might come from listening to the *Jazz at the Ohio Union* concert,[4] which records the Lewis band first as a jazz group and then in an extended demonstration of brass-band playing. The musicians deliberately adopt a different stylistic approach to the brass-band work, especially in terms of part relationships and harmonies. The hymns, dirges, and marches are intoned quite loosely—emphasizing vibrato, a crying tone quality, and much freer rhythmic patterns than in the jazz-band numbers. The brass-band ensemble is radically different from the jazz-band format: there is no tight piano-bass-banjo focus for harmonic and rhythmic patterns, only relation-

A Bourbon Street parade. *Alcide "Slow Drag" Pavageau marshalling the Eureka Brass Band, May 28, 1961. Left to right: Albert Warner, Emanuel Paul, Oscar "Chicken" Henry, Willie Humphrey, Christopher "Black Happy" Goldston. "Every Sunday there was a parade in New Orleans. . . . They would have from two to eight and ten parades on Sunday. I've never seen it so small they only had one."—Jelly Roll Morton, Library of Congress interview (1938).*

ships between "choirs" of wind instruments and the bass drum-snare drum rhythmic cadence. Thus more "holes" appear in the texture of the music, through which different voices emerge for different emphases; this style differs from the conventional "Dixieland" relationship of front-line instruments plus rhythm section, or lead voices contrasted with timekeepers.

The same comparisons can be made of other New Orleans musicians as they play in jazz groups and with brass bands. A conscious shift of style and instrumental technique occurs in street-band work. This appears also in the work of brass-band musicians drafted into jazz bands. Albert Warner, on Bunk Johnson's 1942 *Jazz Information* session, shows a band trombonist's conventionalized attack and repetitive bass line, incongruous in the jazz setting; the same incongruity applies to Bill Matthews' trombone playing with Papa Celestin's band in the 1950s.[5] The brass-band style is distinct from various New Orleans jazz styles, though closely akin. Currents back and forth from jazz playing and brass-band work make it impossible to pinpoint which specific ideas and techniques came first, but there is no doubt that street playing was a musical style with conventions and nuances distinct from jazz. More important, the musicians seemed highly conscious of differences between the way they played brass-band music and the way they played jazz standards.

Another element from the brass-band tradition influencing the course of New Orleans jazz was the rep-ertoire of the bands. Brass-band musicians learned a repertoire of scored marches, funeral dirges, and hymns used on the street, along with dance music and popular tunes. In work with jazz bands, the musicians often used these brass-band tunes. The process was two-way, as brass bands also adopted popular jazz tunes. The flow of ideas was cross-cultural: bandsmen picked up musical ideas from every quarter of the city, from every ethnic group. The presence of the French Opera meant that familiar passages like the sextet from *Lucia* could be rendered as funeral dirges. Overtures were staples in the concert-band repertoire. Folksongs were collected from New Orleans' polyglot community. Other music was taken directly from the standard march repertoire—"High Society" or "My Maryland." Marches were constructed from popular music of the day—as W. H. Tyers' tango "Panama" (1911) was shifted to 2/4 time, ornamented, and made into an enduring brass-band favorite.

An obvious source of the brass bands' repertoires was dance music. Just as the folk music of the region was polyglot and multitraditional—coming from dozens of countries, from isolated ethnic and dialect groups, and from various traditions of religious and social values—so was the tradition of dancing. Rural parishes each had distinct dance fashions. In the city itself were Creoles, Italians, Germans, Irish, West Indians, and a highly stratified community from all over the rural South. Dance orchestras had to know many kinds of music to play for any kind of dancing. The spectrum of nineteenth-century ballroom or cotillion music was represented—waltzes, mazurkas, polkas, two-steps, schottisches, quadrilles, plus hundreds of variants on these decorous dances.

The first implication here is that any band playing for dancing—and many brass bands accompanied dances[6]—had a strong rhythmic sound. Bandsmen had to play energetic and rhythmically consistent dance music through long evenings. They had to play over sounds of dancing crowds and maintain a steady, compelling beat. Secondly, the bands had to know a wide repertoire of music. They also had to be acquainted with the potpourri music used for multipart dances (like the quadrille, lancers, and varieties) popular at the time, in which each dance section was accompanied by a specific musical form in a characteristic tempo and rhythm. This potpourri dance form was a main influence on the medley/multithematic forms of later jazz, as dance tunes were written with three of four distinct strains and contrasting themes.[7] Similarities between the multithematic march and dance forms must have hastened blending of these ideas in the bands' music. Jelly Roll Morton, in describing his "invention" of "Tiger Rag," went through the pattern for the quadrille as black New Orleanians danced it, ca. 1900. He described explicitly how the multisectional dance form led to his multithematic musical structure.[8]

After the turn of the century dances were usually played by dance bands—jazz groups or "sit-down" orchestras reading popular arrangements. But brass bands kept dance music in their repertoires, and later bands would play "Lady Be Good" or "You Tell Me Your Dream" with great swing and *elan*. They would also pick up the latest jukebox favorites of the day—in the 1950s rhythm-and-blues hits like "Work With Me, Annie" or "It Feels So Good" and even novelty tunes like "How Much Is That Doggie in the Window?" These were not reduced to stiff march rhythms, like commercial arrangements for college marching bands, but played with the same rhythmic feeling a dance band would intuitively adopt. The dance feeling is one of the strongest elements of the New Orleans street-band sound, an element permeating the music and communicating itself to the second liners following the band. The followers never march in four-square fashion; they shuffle and strut. And the dance impulse is the fabric of this music.

Perhaps the single largest source of music for the brass bands was the church. Hymnals of Baptist and Methodist churches and many fundamentalist sects provided an inexhaustible font of music familiar to the bandsmen and their audiences. The advantage of this familiarity is obvious, considering that some musicians were "ear-trained." Hymns and spirituals like "Bye and Bye," "Over in the Gloryland," "Sing On" and "Lord, Lord, Lord" were brilliantly suited for brass playing—as was other semifolk music from evangelistic black churches, pieces like "The Royal Telephone." Through the pervasive influence of the

The George Williams Brass Band *in an Uptown funeral, September 5, 1964. Left to right: Henry "Pickle" Jackson, Henry "Booker T" Glass, Joseph Bentley, Theodore Riley, Sam Alcorn, Herman Sherman, Joseph "Brother Cornbread" Thomas, Bill Brown, Albert Warner, Louis Nelson. "The band would start, why we know that the man was fixin' to be buried, so you could hear the band come up the street, be-* *fore they would get to the place where the gentleman was to be taken for his last rites, and they would play different dead marches. And on leavin', this would be the march they would usually start to playin': 'Flee As a Bird to the Mountain.'" —Jelly Roll Morton, Library of Congress interview (1938).*

brass bands, some of this music became effectively secularized. In 1927 a popular New Orleans group, Sam Morgan's Jazz Band, recorded "Sing On," "Over in the Gloryland," and "Down By the Riverside"—a revolutionary moment, since earlier it had been considered sacrilegious for a popular group to play such music outside a church context. The continual rendering of this music in the streets by brass bands, often in a distinctly jazzy vein, helped to pass it into the language of popular music in America. This is most obvious in the case of the most ubiquitous hymn, "When the Saints Go Marching In," recorded by Louis Armstrong in 1938 as an example of New Orleans street-band music. The hymn has now become the anthem of traditional jazz in the popular imagination, and most people dissociate it from religious roots.

An example of brass-band music developed as popular musical material is shown by King Oliver's Creole Jazz Band, the first black New Orleans group to make a series of distinguished and characteristic recordings of the city's jazz. In 1923 and 1924 Oliver's band made several recordings for Gennett, Paramount, Columbia, and other companies; and the bandsmen were drawn largely from brass-band veterans. Joe Oliver himself had made his reputation when he joined Manuel Perez in the Onward Brass Band; Johnny and Baby Dodds had years of experience with many bands; Honore Dutrey was familiar with the trombone idiom of the street bands; Louis Armstrong joined Oliver in 1922 and was still much in love with memories of New Or-

leans street playing. The Creole Jazz Band is our best example of the transition New Orleans jazzmen made from brass-band playing to the dance-band style.

Most of the music Oliver recorded in 1923 and 1924 was original material, but it was closely related to the march/ragtime music of the street bands. This is especially apparent in tunes like "Buddy's Habits," "Chattanooga Stomp," "New Orleans Stomp," and "Snake Rag"—essentially marches with three contrasting strains and careful polyphonic relationships between lead instruments. The hymn influence shines through an Oliver composition like "Camp Meeting Blues," which captures the sound of the churches and connects it with secular blues sounds. The same relationships are evident in "Workingman Blues" or "Chimes Blues" (which introduces "The Holy City," a favorite trumpet solo in church services) or "Riverside Blues," with their chorale-like construction and close hymn harmonies. But the obvious example of brass-band influence comes in "High Society." This first recording of the Porter Steele tune by a New Orleans band shows how marches melded directly into the jazz-band sound. Edmond Souchon recalled hearing Oliver's band play it at Tulane University about five years before the recording was made.

In order to get the couples into line and stop the dancing, Oliver was requested to play a march to which no one could dance. He would use *High Society*. It was played at a very slow marching tempo, the same tempo his band used in marching funerals and processions. It was a shuffle, easy to walk to. And the first part seemed interminable, before he broke nto the chorus which has immortalized Alphonse Picou. You couldn't even do a "slow drag" to it, as it was played then. Gradually, the tempo of this tune was quickened, and it was converted into a dance tune, almost the same as we know today; the transformation probably took three or four years![9]

As the Creole Jazz Band played it on the three-minute phonograph record of 1923, it is taken at a brisk tempo and sounds like dance music—but the march origins of the tune (and of the musicians) are evident.[10]

The Creole Jazz Band recordings show how a World War I period New Orleans brass band must have played. Since these recordings transmit the sound of the front-line instruments more clearly than the rhythm section (and Oliver used only a three-piece rhythm section behind his four winds), similarities with the brass band are underscored. The two-part cornet harmonies, Johnny Dodds's intricate clarinet obbligatos, Honore Dutrey's foundation part on trombone—all reflect the brass-band experiences from which Oliver and his men had so lately graduated. The band is in transition from New Orleans street music to popular Chicago dance music, but a pervasive influence is the brass band.

This influence recurs through the earliest New Orleans jazz recordings. It runs like a ribbon through the work of the first recording band from the city; records by the Original Dixieland Jazz Band in 1917 and 1918 reflect the training these musicians had had with Jack "Papa" Laine's white brass bands. Many tunes like "Tiger Rag," "Sensation Rag," "Clarinet Marmalade," and "Fidgety Feet" were drawn from the repertoires of Laine's street and tent-show bands, and they exhibit the brass-band styles of Larry Shields's clarinet, Nick LaRocca's cornet, and Eddie Edwards' trombone. Their tunes are on the common march/rag multithematic pattern and played with a stiff march beat (if at exaggeratedly brisk tempos). The relationship of the three lead horns is that of the brass band—with Shields and LaRocca playing lead figures and Edwards building a complex, looping counterpoint around them on trombone, providing in part a tenor countermelody. A tune like "Fidgety Feet" is a syncopated march; it was retitled "War Cloud" at the height of World War I militarism and some twenty-five years later was still played by Kid Howard and his bands as a march.

Jelly Roll Morton, who is remembered as a "professor" or "tickler" in Storyville brothels more than as a bandsman, kept the brass bands' influence in mind throughout his career. A record like his Red Hot Peppers Band's version of "Beale Street Blues" (1927) pays homage to the brass band in a slightly satirical take-off on W. C. Handy's reputation as a "legitimate" bandmaster. At the very beginning (1924) of his band-recording career Morton cut "High Society," as he did at the very end (1939). He also used other brass-band tunes like "Oh, Didn't He Ramble," "Panama," and his own "Swinging the Elks." Many of his original compositions—amalgamations of classic ragtime, barrelhouse blues, pop music, and massive infusions of his own unique genius—echo the street bands of his youth and his occasional career as a street-band drummer or trombonist: "Tanktown Bump," "Shoe-Shiner's Drag," "The Pearls," "Sidewalk Blues," and "Dead Man Blues" (with its explicit imitation of a funeral band) reflect the solid, bouncy beat of the marching band and the free polyphony of its brass-reed choir.

The enlarging repertoire of the jazz band from 1900 to 1920 mirrored the expansion of the repertoire and style of brass bands. The connection is so close as to be organic; and cross-connections between brass bands and jazz bands became so much stronger that distinctions were eventually erased. Only older musicians remembered when brass bands played in a style markedly different from that used by jazz groups of New Orleans.

Still another influence of brass bands was the set of elements of musical style and technique communicated to jazz. This influence took the form of a penchant for highly structured, ceremonial music and a commitment to "functional" instrumental music—for dancing, marching, accompanying specific social occasions. Brass bands habitually played scored music like the standard marches with their three or four strains, repeats, and rigidly constructed counterpoint. They played complex traditional dance forms like the quadrille. They read scores for dirges, often multithematic pieces with contrasting sections, and they included some classic ragtime, another scored multithematic form. All of this was music in the mainstream of nineteenth-century American culture, inclined toward formalism and a characteristic decorum. This aspect of form, ritual, ceremony is the point at which these black brass bands connect most directly with the wind-band traditions of America.

Many early brass bandsmen, when reminiscing about their training, emphasized that reading bands in which they first played used 6/8 marches, waltzes, and music in other meters—but rarely the 2/4 "split" time associated with jazz. They asserted that jazz in this swinging march meter was a late addition to the brass-band style. Some older marches still used by street bands are, in fact, in 6/8 time (e.g., "Salutation March," "Gettysburg March," and Bunk Johnson's march version of "Oh, Didn't He Ramble"). New Orleans snare-drum cadences, used between numbers on parade, were often in 6/8 rather than duple meter. The shift to 2/4 put the bands into the meter of ragtime and the new syncopated popular music, but the early march repertoire and the 6/8 cavalry meter never disappeared. This part of the marching band heritage remains a submerged feeling in jazz—the springy, relaxed beat, at a comfortable walking cadence.[11]

Brass bands normally played for marching and for processions, providing music with a regular marching tempo. Even dirge music was designed for a slow walk or stylized shuffle. When the bands played for

In shade and sunshine—*the Young Excelsior Brass Band on the Tulane campus in 1964. Left to right: "Sleepy" Robertson, Leon Vageon, Carroll Blunt, Louis Keppard, John Wimberly, "Buster" Moore, Leroy Robinet.*

dancing, they provided a clear, even rhythm—often several specific kinds of rhythm, as in "set" dances like the quadrille. The bands were expected to provide a background for particular social functions, and they were expected to know music for many public occasions. These occasions were often outdoors, against noisy, active backgrounds, and the bands developed a powerful rhythmic thrust, a loud, singing style to carry across city streets, parks, and large, packed dance halls. Bandsmen were accustomed to blowing long and loud, everyone playing at once, through every number, for four or five hours.

But the main idea bandsmen absorbed from their routines of playing was that of using complex, multi-thematic music in dense ensembles. This built a foundation for early jazz bands like King Oliver's, which would also play this music, usually in sketchy head arrangements rather than from scores, for four or five hours in big Chicago dance palaces. It made development of new tunes from bits and pieces of old ones habitual, so that the Original Dixieland Jazz Band used themes from Laine tunes, copyrighted them, and gave them catchy novelty titles—"Bluin' the Blues," "Tiger Rag" (the latter was called by a dozen names in New Orleans: "No. 2," "Meatball," "Jack Carey," "Snotsy"), "Skeleton Jangle." Much of the music brass bandsmen played was potpourri music—three or four themes linked together loosely for contrast. Even some printed dirges were really potpourris: several different dirge melodies laced together in contrasting ar-

rangements, with alternating ensemble and solo passages. Band musicians could remember these melange tunes, even without identifying titles. One practice common among brass bandsmen and early jazzmen was to cut publishers' titles from scores so that rival musicians could not "scout" them and steal successful tunes. Thus, in the Eureka Brass Band, one of the most effective dirges was simply numbered "31" at the tops of the music cards. The Eureka bandsmen nicknamed it "The Blimp" for its ponderous arrangement, but its real title was "Fallen Heroes," and it had once been identified with Manuel Perez' virtuoso cornet playing with the Onward Brass Band.[12]

The habit of working with music more complicated than the usual popular tune—with three or four sections connected and repeated in a set order—shaped the jazz that dominated the 1920s and became known as characteristic New Orleans (then Chicago) jazz. Musicians in this tradition approached music in a complicated way: they were prepared to read straight arrangements, to rely on head arrangements of standard tunes in the repertoire, and to improvise on new tunes. This kind of brass-band playing was not restricted to New Orleans; it occurred in other black communities. And road shows (circuses, vaudeville, minstrelsy) carried brass bands playing in this fashion. Garvin Bushell, a New York jazzman born and reared in Ohio, was trained in this tradition: "I played in *Ol' Kentuck'*, a book show, at 14th Street. We did three shows a day and before each show, we went out front to ballyhoo. We played on the stage and improvised. We didn't have any saxophones; we did have three clarinets, tuba, three trumpets, two trombones, two upright baritone horns, and two drums (bass and snare)."[13] Bushell remembers the brass bands of the circus-vaudeville tradition (*ca.* 1918) as depending on ragtime and popular music for staples: "In the shows, we played and improvised on pop tunes and all of Scott Joplin. Everybody played Scott differently. The main theme would be stated, but then everybody did little things of his own."[14] The spread of this circus-band tradition across the country, often accompanied by New Orleans musicians,[15] followed the nationwide craze for "jass" at the end of World War I.

The black brass bands in New Orleans flowered in the 1880s and 1890s, and by 1900 they had metamorphosed under the wide popular impact of syncopated music. The old tradition of strict reading bands, rigorously schooled to play "legitimate" concert music and highly proper dance tunes, gave way to the influx of a younger generation of musicians who were essentially dance-band oriented and for whom street-band playing was secondary. Both Joe Oliver and Louis Armstrong were jazzmen first and brass-band musicians second, as were many of the first generation of Chicago jazzmen. Yet all this new dance music was sewn together, like a patchwork quilt, of the practices, repertoire, and social functions of older brass bands. Henry Kmen, the most exacting historian of New Orleans music, identified four main attributes of black brass

bands after the Civil War. First, parades of the era were not only formal occasions, but celebratory, "simply to have fun," which dictated the kind of music played on the march—"the atmosphere changed; and the music became less martial, less formal, and acquired more lilt, more swing." Second, black burial societies multiplied, creating a demand for funeral music, which brought religious music into the repertoire of the brass bands. Third, the wide demand for bands both to march and to play in dance halls kept the bands small in size. Fourth, "the brass bands of New Orleans were increasingly used for ballyhoo [advertisement]." This meant they appeared on all occasions, sometimes in combination with nonbrass-band instruments.[16] These characteristics led directly to turn-of-the-century jazz bands and to the brass bands that accompanied the growth of jazz.

The significant point gleaned from this prehistory of jazz is that the brass bands left a deep, ineradicable imprint on the music and that they in turn were shaped and redirected by the immense popularity of jazz. The story of the black brass bands in New Orleans in the twentieth century describes a symbiosis, two musics coexisting and mingling, never quite merging. The brass bands never lost their distinct individuality, their music never quite became identical with that of the dance bands. Following the bands from 1900 to the 1960s, we can see how this symbiosis functioned, what cross-currents kept the mutual traditions together and separate.

In dirge tempo—*Harold Dejan's Olympia Brass Band at Mount Olivet Cemetery, January 22, 1965. Left to right. Albert Warner, Louis Cottrell, Jr., "Kidney Stew," Bill Brown, George Williams, Worthia "Showboy" Thomas, Harold Dejan, Alvin Alcorn.*

To envision a New Orleans parade, on a day in any year from 1900 to 1960, imagine a sunny forenoon in New Orleans, a holiday. On a side street a band forms for a parade. The bandsmen are black; most are in their fifties or sixties. Dressed in white shirts, dark ties and trousers, black shoes, each wears a dark uniform cap, like a policeman's or bus driver's, with a grand name stitched across it in gold thread. The caps are old and worn. The men flutter valves and keys on their horns, blow phrases through them to warm up, adjust tuning slides. There are a couple of trombones, a clarinetist with a stubby E^b instrument, an old Muller-style horn manufactured before the turn of the century, an alto sax, a tenor sax, a bulky Sousaphone, a bass drum with one small cymbal mounted atop it (beaten with a stiff bent wire) and the band's name painted in bold block letters on the left-hand head. There is a snare drummer, with a shallow dance-band drum hitched high on his belly, and there are three trumpets. One trumpet player, the leader, carries a little cloth bag filled with band scores—cards from which the band will read any arranged music. These scores are old and dog-eared; someone has snipped the tops off, removing the titles and the composers' names, and has numbered them instead—51, 31, 209.

Today's parade, sponsored by a social-aid and pleasure club, is an annual marching excursion. The club members plan to parade up and down the streets of this district all afternoon, stopping at taverns and cafes for interludes of rest and refreshment. Club members are dressed neatly in suits and fancy dresses, with bright sashes and emblems decorating them. Some of the women carry parasols, trimmed with sequins, fringe, or feathers. One man holds a silky banner embroidered with the club's name and the date of its founding. The grand marshall for the parade, president of the social-aid and pleasure club, wears a wide sash across his breast, with the club's name spelled out in florid type; the sash is embellished with sequins and glitter. Club members line up and the band falls into a loose formation ahead of them. Marching order for the band is:

	TBN.	CLT.		TPT.	S.D.
← MARSHALL	TBN.	TENOR SAX		TPT.	
	BASS	ALTO SAX		TPT.	B.D.

(The Eureka Brass Band often marched the trumpets *behind* the drums, to put the rhythm in the middle and steady the band's beat.)

As the parade forms, passersby stop to watch. Neighborhood children assemble with the procession. News of the impending celebration passes quickly, and everyone is ready for holiday fun. Sunlight sparkles off the polished horns, the sequined emblems and banners. Everything contributes to a gala feeling that something joyful is about to happen.

With order established among the marchers, the grand marshall nods to the band. Bandsmen cease tuning up and fidgeting. The leader signals the snare drummer, who strikes up a cadence. The shallow, high-tuned snare drum rings thinly in the open air, but the cadence is audible across the procession:

The parade starts uncertainly. No one is exactly marching, but each parader tries to walk in step with the cadence. Children group themselves loosely ahead of the band and marchers, along the sidewalks (called *banquettes* in New Orleans) on both sides of the street. This is the "second line" inevitably accompanying a parade—impromptu marchers and dancers along to enjoy free music and celebration. And this second line is by no means limited to children; enthusiasts of all ages escort the band. The second liners will spill off the sidewalks when the parade warms up, capering before the band and parodying the dignified but lively posture of the grand marshall, threatening to clog the thoroughfare. The grand marshall will deal with them, keeping them clear of the parade, preventing them from spoiling the ceremonial beauty of the occasion. If pressed he will threaten to stop the band and call off the parade—a threat never carried out but always potent.

As the procession moves to the high, buzzing rhythm of the snare drum, everyone is ready for music. After a moment's march, the band leader signals the musicians to prepare to play. On the march the leader (a trumpet player) is the musical director. Although the grand marshall guides the parade, he has nothing to do with setting tempos or conducting the band. The leader signals for the band to begin playing and designates the tunes to be used; the snare drummer controls the marching tempo with his cadence interludes, the "street beat." By blowing on his trumpet the leader alerts the band, using a little bugle-call and three or four notes of the tune to be played. The first number in today's imaginary parade will be the grand old New Orleans march "Panama":

Trumpet Introduction to "Panama"—in E♭

The snare drummer knows that at the end of his cadence he must roll off to start the band. The roll-off he uses is different from that of the standard military bands, but it works the same way to move from marching cadence into the march's introduction. He plays two measures of a 6/8 figure, to which the bass drum responds with three loud beats:

The roll-off sets the tempo. It begins on the snare drum and ends on the bass drum, whose set of sharp raps pushes the band into the first measures of the march.

The band bursts into the opening measures of "Panama," uniformly delighting the paraders, the spectators, and the second liners. With the beginning of the music, the procession is animated. Four bars of a fanfare-like figure prepare everyone for the dance-like feeling of the music. Plunging into the music at full volume, the brass-band sound rolls and echoes in the narrow street above the noise of the marchers. More second liners and spectators appear like magic. Now almost everyone within four or five blocks hears the parade, and has time to spare, stepping onto stoops, popping out of taverns, strolling around corners from adjacent streets.

The parade gathers headway, and the marchers' joy is proportionate to the volume and intensity of the band's cross-rhythms. Through the first two strains, the dancing and strutting are relatively restrained; but when the band winds up on the famous last strain, the bass drummer shifts from two beats per measure to four and the trumpets soar up into a series of chime-like descending tones—a variation on the original melody supposedly written by "Professor" Manuel Manetta around the beginning of World War I for the semilegendary trumpeter Emmett Hardy, now the traditional last chorus for "Panama." Marchers along the street and sidewalk ahead of the band outdo themselves in elaborate dance steps, high-kicking struts, ecstatic leaps. The lead trumpet squeals over unison trombone riffs and counter-riffs by the saxes, all floating on Sousaphone on-beats and the on-and-off syncopations of snare and bass drums.[17] The march ends like a thunderclap; there is a second of silence and echoes, then the snare drum goes back to its cadence placidly, as if nothing had disturbed it.

The parade snakes down narrow streets, across intersections, stopping traffic, the grand marshall leading with stolid decorum. He walks with dignity, undistracted by capering second liners, by passersby shouting and pointing. He guides the parade along the route he has selected, and often when he reaches an intersection he moves more than halfway through it before making a turn with the procession. This is a time-honored method for feinting and losing the second line, which moves ahead of the band, guessing at its route. After a few minutes' marching to the ringing snare-drum cadence, almost lost in the mob's noise, the leader again blows his warning call, this time indicating another familiar tune, a march adaptation of the blues, called variously "Holler Blues" or "Whoopin' Blues."[18] This favorite demands audience participation. It incorporates a stop-time section, requiring a vocal break in the form of an *ad libitum* shout from band and audience. The snare drummer ends his cadence, switches into a 6/8 measure of the roll-off; the bass drum enters with its three resonant thumps, and the band comes in again *ff*.

When the band reaches the stop-time figure introducing the audience's shout, tension rises until the break comes and everyone shouts. The sharp punctuations of the bass drum in the stop-time section build up to the "release" of the yell itself. The music goes on, trumpets shouting traditional blues-changes over a modified boogie-woogie bass line from Sousaphone and trombones—a *marching*, not just a *walking*, bass —and saxophone riffs. The social-aid and pleasure club marchers strut. Ahead of them, the second liners have caught up again and fill the street with leaping, capering figures. Kids dance, using old black umbrellas as drum-major's batons. The opened umbrella is stood on its ferule in the street as a centerpiece (as in a hat- or sword-dance) around which the dancers gyrate. The grand marshall gestures the second liners out of the route, but while the band grinds through "Whoopin' Blues" it is difficult to stop the crowd. Reaching the stop-time section again, the band drives through the sharp stop-figures, then reaches the shout, which rises with a raw whoop and then fades off; the band has stopped! The trick ending never fails to surprise the listener, the sudden silence seeming as loud as any *fff* accent.

The snare drum picks up the cadence in the silence, and the procession moves on. It reaches a first resting place—a small neighborhood restaurant-bar—and the marchers swarm from the street for a few minutes in the cool tavern. Band members move out of the crowd, sheltering their instruments from the jostling. They go in for a beer and a sandwich before the long afternoon on the winding streets.

The bandsmen sit in the shade of the porch, drinking beer or soft drinks and exchanging quiet small talk. They are sweaty and tired from the sun, but they are ready for a hard walk and a lot of playing, the usual parade routine. Their crushed uniform caps bear an exultant name: *Excelsior, Eureka, Onward, Olympia, Zenith*, or *Banner*—a name suggesting excellence or striving, natural in a city whose streets, districts, and institutions are famous for grand, mellifluous names.[19] The city boasts streets named after the muses—Terpsichore, Clio, Melpomene—and after the arts themselves—Music, Literature. Other thoroughfares carry moralistic and euphonious names: Industry, Prosperity, Mandolin, Hope, Law, Pleasure. The social clubs and benevolent associations have traditionally used exalted, poetic titles. The Eureka Benevolent Society, for instance, was established in 1866.[20] And tradesmen adopted these names as freely as the secret orders and societies. *Woods Classified Colored Business, Professional and Trade Directory* for 1912 lists two Eureka barber shops (the Eureka Shaving Saloon and the Eureka Shaving Parlor), an Onward Shaving Parlor, and an Old Reliable Barber Shop.[21] A Eureka Hall once stood at the corner of Bienville and Pelican streets.[22] There was a Eureka Guards organization;[23] and there was an Onward Circle existing as a social club connected with the Larendon Rifles drill team and an Onward Benevolent Association.[24] The brass bands of New Orleans come honestly by their grand names and traditions. Here, as elsewhere in America, the band tradition tapped a profound native feeling for exaltation and pomp.[25]

Both the names and the uniforms reflected the formal feelings the community invested in the bands.[26] These were not raggle-taggle "jump-up" bands assembled impromptu for one afternoon's fun. They were musical organizations with a long heritage of musical achievement. They appeared every year on special days; Labor Day, Odd Fellows' Day, almost any occasion would draw them out. They played regularly for benevolent association burials, for Masonic processions and rituals, for church parades, political rallies. Some musicians marched with the same band for fifty years, playing the same music throughout that period. Old-time musicians like Isidore Barbarin, Bunk Johnson, and Sunny Henry worked from near the beginning of the band tradition to near its end. The bandsmen, like municipal musicians in Renaissance Europe, were invested with an important civic duty in playing their music and passing on their musical traditions and techniques to succeeding generations.

Regardless of how worn the old uniform caps are, the band's proud name is still visible, painted on the outside bass drum head (perhaps with a telephone number, so that potential customers can contact the group for future jobs).

When the procession reforms, properly refreshed and exuberant, the drummer starts his cadence; the band moves off and within a block strikes up another march. The brassy sound in the narrow streets, under dense foliage, and before rows of small, close-cramped houses, is still the sound of surprise. It is easy to imagine the impact these early jazz bands must have had on their first audiences. Hearing the music now recalls an early ad for the Original Dixieland Jazz Band in 1917, a few months after their first New York recordings:

"A brass band gone crazy!"

That's the way a wag describes the original Dixieland "Jass" Band. Beyond that description we can't tell you what a "Jass" Band is because we don't know ourselves.

As for what it *does*—it makes dancers want to dance more —and more—and yet more! Just have another look at the picture above—you can almost *hear* the hilarious music of the "Jass" Band in your ears.

You'll want to hear the first Victor Record by this organized disorganization—it's a "winner." "Livery Stable Blues," a fox trot, and "Dixieland Jass Band One-Step" are played with charming ferocity and penetration.[27]

Even in this antiquated ad-man's hyperbole some words are telling: "organized disorganization," "charming ferocity and penetration." This is still the paradoxical way that street-band music may strike an unprepared listener—as a mixture of apparently incompatible materials magically cemented by ensemble style. The Original Dixieland Jazz Band was perhaps only a white ragtime-and-hokum band that

Marching to a dirge cadence—*the Eureka Brass Band, October 10, 1964. Left to right: Albert Warner, Chester Jones, Oscar "Chicken" Henry, Jerry Greene, Andrew Morgan, "Kid Shiek" Colar.*

stumbled into success through an accident of show business, but its first widely sold records were stunning and revelatory to America.

That freshness meets the ear in a New Orleans parade—an excitement never captured on recordings. It is a *social* excitement, with dancing, laughing people, under a canopy of musical sound—and a *musical* excitement, with criss-crossing instrumental lines, complex rhythms, and dense sonic texture. Any live music in congenial surroundings manufactures a gestalt more complex than the sum of its parts, and this is particularly true of this community-created music in its own milieu. A listener might experience the elation young Charles Ives felt in New England at a holiday parade in the 1880s, when several village bands passed him in full cry and he heard the beautifully dissonant collisions of sound. Or one might share the feelings William Russell described in New Orleans in 1945: "Then they [the Eureka Brass Band] marched back on Iberville up to Claiborne & down to about St. Louis, where they ran into another O[dd] F[ellows] parade. The other group stopped & opened up to let the Eureka band turn left and pass thru it. Both bands continued playing their pieces—ff—at different tempos. . . . Wished I had my tape recorder there to catch it. The Eureka played Bye & Bye & got thru OK, & seemed to pep up & play their very best for the next few blocks."[28] The concatenation of sounds in a parade might at first be disturbing just as the loose polyphony of one band might seem at first "barbarous" or "sloppy"; but there is no denying the first principle of rhythm. The energy of street bands is inescapable.

The parade will run its course, winding around the town, returning to its headquarters, where the day will end with a dinner-dance and celebration by any paraders still on their feet. The music of the band will be gone, except for echoes in the mind.

In recent years brass bands have been connected with the jazz revival centered around the "kitty halls" that have flourished since the 1960s, especially Preservation Hall. These kitty halls were informal places where audiences were encouraged to donate tips to supplement the bands' pay. The last decades have seen subtle transformations of the bands' roles. Late nineteenth-century brass bands developed in a sub-subculture. They were musical auxiliaries for benevolent associations, drill teams, baseball clubs; and they principally provided music for organization meetings and functioned as social organizations themselves. Bands like those on Magnolia plantation or Jack Laine's groups developed for musical or entrepreneurial reasons. But they were still connected with social clubs, fraternal organizations, and the like. Bands in the years following the Great Depression were less directly tied to social groups, except through individual musicians' connections.

By the 1960s many of these ties had withered. Bands were as likely to perform as specimens of New Orleans jazz for "concert" situations as to play for ceremonies within the black community. These "specimen" performances are not just commercial exploitation, though exposure through television, films, and concert appearances has allowed the bands to drift away from the older repertoire and style. New outlets like kitty halls, banquet-concert jobs, and other "indoor" work have kept brass bands playing, and in fact the 1960s saw revival of brass bands. The revived Onward Brass Band and Harold Dejan's Olympia Brass Band fostered interest in street bands and their functions. Earlier revived bands like the Young Tuxedo Brass Band (functioning from the 1930s through the early 1960s) sparked enthusiasm among listeners and performers. Musicians like John Casimir, who led the Young Tuxedo Brass Band, and Paul Barbarin, who directed the Onward Brass Band, had roots deep in the history of New Orleans brass bands; and they sought musicians steeped in those same traditions. They inducted younger men and helped to keep bands organized through the 1960s.

Individual musicians have also provided continuity. Musicians like Willie Pajaud, Sunny Henry, and Peter Bocage of the Eureka Brass Band link other bands in the tradition, a family affair as well as part of neighborhood subculture. Family names like Barbarin, Cottrell, Tio, Dutrey, Baquet, Humphrey, Brunies, and others recur throughout histories of individual bands and of the whole brass-band movement. Largely a spontaneous amateur phenomenon, organized for fun, not profit, the brass-band movement was built on a love of spectacle and drama as much as on musical interests. Sheltered within small neighborhoods and districts, playing this music was considered finally something people "just did." Many bandsmen did not consider themselves musicians; they played in brass bands for sheer love of a holiday outing. "Black Benny" Williams, one of the most famous bass drummers with 1920s bands, is an example. A happy-go-lucky man of a "Sportin' Life" cast, his brass-band drumming was his most notable musical venture. Henry Allen, Sr., a long-time leader, kept bands going for almost half a century simply because he enjoyed brass-band work, though he was an indifferent trumpet player and rarely worked outside his own brass band in Algiers. Other bandsmen were all-round professional musicians—e.g., John Robichaux, who continued drumming with the Excelsior Brass Band long after he became the city's most successful "society" bandleader. Many bands were formed of amateur nonunion musicians who did little or no work outside the brass-band setting. The E. Gibson Brass Band is the best recent example of a group comprised almost totally of nonunion musicians. With bandsmen ranging in age from Dave Bailey, bass drummer, in his seventies, down to Eddie Noble, trombonist, in his twenties, this band is one that played from the 1940s through the mid-1960s as a neighborhood band in New Orleans' Garden District.

This casualness has meant that bands varied enormously in quality and stability. Only a few bands held together over many decades, maintaining a reputation for good musicianship and reliability. Enduring names like the Excelsior Brass Band (1880–1931), the Onward Brass Band (1885–1930), the Tuxedo Brass Band (1910–1925), the Allen Brass Band (1907–1950), and the Eureka Brass Band (1920—) have survived decades of change, maintained stable membership, and kept a distinguished repertoire and reputation. In some cases the bands' longevity might have been accidental, but generally it can be attributed to the tenacity of older musicians preserving tradition. Most brass bands that survived worked hard at it—with regular rehearsals aimed toward careful musicianship and with a sense of pride and proprietorship.

The Depression and World War II dislocated some of these traditions. Those were bitter years for working musicians; the earliest brass bands dissolved, and many bandsmen quit playing. Even the existence of a large, skilled Works Progress Administration (WPA) concert band, ably directed by musicians like Pinchback Touro and Louis Dumaine,[29] could not keep brass bandsmen at work. Manuel Perez put away his cornet in 1937, a half-dozen years after the demise of the Onward Brass Band, with which he had long been closely associated. Bandsmen like Kid Rena and Kid Howard kept brass bands going sporadically, and John Casimir organized the Young Tuxedo Brass Band during the 1930s; but the tradition was fractured. In the early 1940s some bandsmen joined service bands and kept in practice, but the last two decades of the first half of this century saw a decline in the band movement.

However, the blossoming New Orleans jazz revival of the mid-1940s stimulated interest in bands. William Russell made the first recordings of a New Orleans street band in 1945, when he organized a pick-up group including Bunk Johnson and the musicians who had been associated with him for several years—George Lewis, Baby Dodds, Jim Robinson, Lawrence Marrero—and several long-time brass-band veterans—"Kid Shots" Madison, Red Clark, Isidore Barbarin, and Adolphe Alexander. Bunk's Brass Band existed basically only for recording purposes, though it included men associated with outstanding street bands—Red Clark was a Eureka Brass Band regular, Isidore Barbarin's career stretched back to the turn of the century, and Kid Howard led another brass band that Lewis and Robinson played in. This latter group made the second set of brass-band recordings in 1946, when Rudi Blesh organized a session around Kid Howard and named it the Original Zenith Brass Band. These recordings—Russell's on the American Music label and Blesh's on Circle Records—were revelations for record collectors and jazz fans who had read about brass bands but had never heard one. For the first time, this unique New Orleans sound reached listeners around the world.

Not until 1951 was a regularly organized brass band recorded, when two young men, Alden Ashforth and David Wycoff, taped the Eureka Brass Band. Some three-quarters of a century after the inception of black brass bands in New Orleans, the outside world paid enough attention to document their work. Following these initial recordings, serious efforts to capture the brass bands' sounds were made in the fifties and sixties. Samuel Charters recorded the Eureka Brass Band again in 1956 and 1958 for Folkways Records. Atlantic Records, the only large firm interested in the genre, recorded the Young Tuxedo Brass Band in 1958; this album was elaborate and widely promoted. Atlantic in 1962 recorded the Eureka band in a project documenting revived musicians associated with Preservation Hall. Other recordings have been made by small jazz-speciality houses with limited promotion and distribution. This constitutes the electronic documentation, aside from television and sound-track recordings, of our Afro-American musical tradition.

Street bands were acknowledged in the lore of jazz. Beginning with the pioneering study *Jazzmen* in 1939, every history of jazz has mentioned the brass-band tradition and its part in the development of jazz. Many of these discussions were cursory; some were even inaccurate in assumptions and conclusions. Brass bands have generally been treated as remote prototypical ancestors of jazz, ancient archetypes from which genuine jazz grew by a mysterious process of transmutation. In reality, the brass-band tradition has been continuous, has indeed coexisted with jazz. The lack of documentation in sound has made critical

Photo courtesy F. Jack Hurley

Bereavement paraphernalia—*banners of the Young and True Friends Benevolent Association of Carrollton and the Merry-Go-Round Social and Aid Club of New Orleans, with furled U.S. flags for funeral use.*

and historical commentaries vague or incomplete; the tendency to assume that *old* means *ancestral* has created confusion. One recent essay on jazz history demonstrates this critical ambiguity, moving from implicit assumptions to general conclusions without adequate explanation.

In 1959, Charles Edward Smith, in an essay entitled "New Orleans and Traditions in Jazz,"[30] collected background materials of jazz and discussed approaches to them. Smith wrote under the impact of the recently released (1958) Young Tuxedo Brass Band album and other recordings of the 1950s, and he made erroneous assumptions about the music on these discs. In a sense Smith came to the right conclusions for the wrong reasons. He described brass bands as carriers of musical tradition in New Orleans:

Traditional ways of brass-band playing continue in the present decade because the brass bands (and their repertoire, like that of the country brass bands, as Frederic Ramsey, Jr., has noted) represented a continuity of the nineteenth century, when ancestors of the bands' members played in groups that pre-dated even the original Tuxedo. . . . *Though jazz changed radically beginning with the Chicago period of almost forty years ago* (some New Orleans men who were a part of all that went back home), *the music of the brass bands went on as it had in the past, changing only gradually* [italics in original].[31]

To draw these conclusions from the 1958 Young Tuxedo Brass Band recordings is misleading, for that recording reflects almost the opposite case—showing essentially how a "modern" street band adapts itself to the time and place. This disc features some highly traditional elements: carefully read potpourri-dirges in the old funeral style ("Medley of Hymns" and "Eternal Peace"), the standard version of "Panama" as a jazz march, several hymns in funeral-procession style. But it also included a 1950s rhythm-and-blues hit, "It Feels So Good," and many numbers are rendered in a style loosely adapted from swing bands and big rhythm-and-blues groups, with saxophone section-work and riffs reflecting these musical ideas plus work by reeds and brass much like the standard big-band music of the 1930s and 1940s—riffing saxes, growling, screaming trumpets, call-and-response figures closer to Count Basie than to fundamentalist churches. Tunes like "Joe Avery's Piece" and John Casimir's "Whoopin' Blues" project the feeling of the 1950s for down-home, funky rhythm and blues, at the very moment when this music turned into more commercially laced-in rock and roll.

Street bands have mirrored the current tastes of their communities, and jukebox favorites and pop standards have turned up as often as ancient marches and hymns. The style of the bands changed perceptibly in the 1950s, as older brassmen dropped away from regular playing and saxophones replaced the old alto-baritone horn section. Whereas older bands were trained in and accustomed to a solid ensemble style demanding iron lips and middle-range playing, younger bandsmen invented new style strategies. Trumpets

A solemn funeral parade, *with the Eureka Brass Band, September 28, 1961. Left to right: Oscar "Chicken" Henry, Bill Matthews, Wilbert Tillman, Willie Humphrey, Robert Lewis, Peter Booage. "Six eight [marches], one-step, quick-step—they'd play all different kinds of mu-* *sic, you understand . . . like them six-eights, them fellows used to play that stuff, you know; take twelve of them men and play just as much as a big symphony orchestra." Jim Robinson, William Ransom Hogan Jazz Archive interview, December 10, 1958, p. 6.*

were less likely to carry a continuous lead; sometimes they dropped out altogether, allowing saxophones and trombones to play the melody. Solos, section-work, and riffing counter-figures replaced some of the old *cantabile* trumpet melodies, so that trumpet men could rest and come in for screaming upper-register final choruses without wrecking their embouchures.

There is more change on the Young Tuxedo record-ings than Smith indicated. To make a flat statement about "traditional ways of brass-band playing" with-out noting that the styles were radically altered by big swing bands, bop experimentation, and rhythm-and-blues jukebox trends overlooks what happens on the Atlantic recording and what is most interesting about it. (This error is encouraged by the packaging of the album, entitled *Jazz Begins*, with a cover illustra-tion of a brass band of *ca*. 1900.) Comparing the disc with the Russell and Blesh recordings of the mid-1940s reveals much about this change; whereas Bunk Johnson, George Lewis, Kid Howard, and their co-horts produced a fairly straightforward march-hymn style, the Young Tuxedo Brass Band recording more accurately depicts what a working brass band (as dis-tinct from a recording pick-up group) played for its regular community audience. *This* is the value of the Young Tuxedo recording and records of the Eureka Brass Band made about the same time. Finally re-cordings began to capture in documentary fashion what bands sounded like on the job, in their own milieu.

Yet even the earliest recordings came late in the tradition. Although Bunk's Brass Band included such staunch old-line bandsmen as Isidore Barbarin, Red Clark, and Adolphe Alexander, as well as younger men like Jim Robinson and Kid Shots Madison who had been seasoned by much street work, and even though Bunk and William Russell tried to replicate an old-time brass-band sound, the disc remains a recording of 1945, not 1905. Distinctly jazzy elements occur in every measure, even in a 6/8 march like "Oh, Didn't He Ramble?" or a hymn like "Nearer My God to Thee." And we do not know if this is how a turn-of-the-century band played. The same discrepancy is even clearer on the 1946 Original Zenith Brass Band re-cordings, which further emphasize the jazz repertoire and style—again, even though they included Isidore Barbarin, Harrison Barnes, Joe Howard, and Peter Bocage, all veterans of "straight" reading bands. The 1946 fashion was different from that of 1905, and the bandsmen undoubtedly knew what kind of music Russell and Blesh collected in New Orleans. Jazz had come to stay in the first decades of the century, and there was no going back to pre-jazz attitudes and hab-its of playing. Even a musician like Peter Bocage, who preferred playing from scores and reading strictly, al-ways played with a lilting, swinging touch, an infec-tious sense of rhythmic drive and momentum.[32] To reconstruct or reassemble musical styles from two generations back was probably impossible, even in 1946 when many veterans were still playing.

Recordings by the Eureka and Young Tuxedo bands in the next decade make this clear. The Eureka bandsmen, especially, steered by leader Percy Humphrey and manager Red Clark, maintained a sense of tradition and decorum in their band style.[33] Even when they used saxophones to replace the scarce alto and baritone horns, musicians like Emanuel Paul tried to duplicate the old horn parts on the reed instruments. And the reed playing on the dirges recorded in 1951 shows how saxes could read the important horn parts and achieve a lyrical and dignified style. The two potpourri-dirges recorded—"West Lawn Dirge" and "Garlands of Flowers"—feature solo saxophone work almost as much as trumpet leads, and the playing of Emanuel Paul and Ruben Roddy is precise and tasteful. But the 1950s recordings still show changes from traditions described by veterans. Aside from the dirges and one circus-style trombone rag ("Trombonium," recorded in 1958), most music was not read but played from head arrangements. Granted, the Eureka bandsmen constructed careful arrangements and rehearsed them tightly; but this was still "ear" music, as opposed to a repertoire on band cards. The Young Tuxedo recordings of 1958 reflect this trend away from printed arrangements even more. Although the band reads several dirges, the recording focuses on "ratty" music, head arrangements in jazz style.

There is no going back, and perhaps there should not even be a desire to go back. This is the authenticity in recordings of New Orleans brass bands: they transmit the musical positions of the bands and also their heritage. We have enough on discs to understand where the bands stood late in their careers and perhaps enough to guess at what they were like in the golden age.

Chapter III **Garlands of Flowers**

After the sermon's over, they'd take the body to the cemetery with the band playing the funeral marches—maybe *Nearer My God to Thee*.

Them oldtime drummers, they just put a handkerchief under the snare on their drums and it go *tunk-a*, *tunk-a*, like a tom-tom effect. And when that body's in the ground, man, tighten up on them snares and he rolls that drum and everybody gets together and they march back to their hall playing *When the Saints* or *Didn't He Ramble*. They usually have a keg of beer back there and they rejoice, you know, for the dead.

> —Louis Armstrong, quoted in Richard Meryman
> *Louis Armstrong—A Self-Portrait*

THE ONE FACT everyone knows about the New Orleans brass bands is that they played for funerals. This may be the only idea firmly associated with the bands, as if they existed for one specialized purpose, bit-players waiting for a walk-on part in a pageant of jazz. But funeral processions were only one duty of the bands, though they did epitomize the bands' work. Funerals were the ultimate ceremony, summarizing the impulse toward social-clubbing, fraternity, celebration, and ritual in the community. Benevolent or burial associations that New Orleans blacks joined offered burial insurance, as well as other forms of assistance and social coherence. But their final obligation was to sponsor a decent, decorous burial for their dues-paying members.

Part of this burial contract included, at the request of the member and his family, music for the funeral, which might mean a band for the funeral cortege. Not all association members chose musical embellishment; some even held religious scruples against music in funeral rites. But members often requested a band as a component of the perfect funeral. The band headed the procession—preceding the hearse, mourners, and members of the association—to add a solemn, splendid weight to the cortege. The band was engaged to provide appropriate music—hymns and dirges—for the procession, to play outside the church or home where the funeral sermon was preached, to accompany the corpse to the graveyard, and to provide hymns or spirituals at the graveside in the ceremony conducted by the deceased's church. The band was central to the religious and social ceremony of the funeral, as specified by the deceased and his family; it was never an improvised or indecorous element interjected into the obsequies, as is sometimes implied in romanticized accounts.

The musical funeral complemented the attitude toward death in the black community—rounding out a ceremonial farewell, a celebration of life as much as a recognition of the triumph of death. As in many cultures, the funeral concluded a period of mixed mourning and rejoicing. Wakes, church services, and hymnsings were part of the process of saying goodbye to the dead, following an ancient Christian practice of crying at the birth and rejoicing at the death. Rejoicing was basic to the funeral, but it was not impromptu or undignified rejoicing. The celebration tried to show that "death is swallowed up in victory," that the end of life is not despair but hope in the resurrection. Powerful religious impulses informed funerals, Protestant and Catholic, whether they were dominated by a religious sect or conducted by a fraternal society like the Masons or Odd Fellows. The roots were in Christian symbolism and liturgy, under whatever banners; and brass bands were central to the elaborate ceremonial display that New Orleans funerals achieved over two hundred years.

Antecedents for ceremonial wind music in funerals occur in French culture (see Berlioz' *Funeral and Triumphal Symphony* and the copious literature of French band dirges), in military and folk traditions of many nationalities (New Orleans has always been a military center, with garrisons for regular troops and militia basic to the city's life), in the wind-band traditions of Moravians and other missionary groups in the early South. Many models exist for the use of bands in New Orleans funerals, so many that it is impossible to designate ancestral sources precisely. Occasional large corteges with band music occurred in the German, Italian, and French communities of New Orleans. Funeral and memorial ceremonies combined military and religious music and ritual.[1] Even the Irish community, low on the city's social scale and solidly Catholic, observed musical funeral customs:

There might or might not be a band in the cortege, depending on whether or not the deceased had belonged to certain organizations. If he had, the music played en route to the cemetery would be low and mournful. Returning from the cemetery, livelier numbers were in order—spritely Irish tunes or popular music of the day—"Good-bye, My Honey, I'm Gone" and "Won't You Come Home, Bill Bailey?"[2]

Editing out a few words in this quotation would make

a classic description of a black New Orleans funeral procession.

Whatever the antecedents of the black funeral practices, the formula itself was established before 1900, and the use of small street bands was commonplace thereafter. The custom was not exclusively black. Early white bandsmen recalled playing for white funerals in much the same manner, with the same routine, as the black bands. Jack Laine made funerals a part of his groups' regular work.[3] One of his bandsmen, Johnny Lala, recalled the demise of the custom among New Orleans whites: "We even played funerals over in Gretna. . . . Brass band, yes sir. They cut it out because soon as we'd leave the cemetery we start playin' the ragtime music, you know, and the families would see that, cryin' and ever'thing. . . . We used to play 'Ballin' the Jack' and all that. Man them people, them sad people that leave—lose the poor unfortunate dead, the wife and children seen all that, of course they cut it out."[4]

However long or widely the custom prevailed in the white community—and it was probably exceptional there—brass-band music for associational funerals in the black community was common for some forty years of the twentieth century. Red Clark of the Eureka Brass Band estimated that he had played for five hundred funerals. There was no hesitation about impropriety, because bands were part of the religious formula. Even ragtime interludes after interment could be viewed as fitting reminders of rejoicing at the death, not as offenses against community decorum or the bereaved. Left to their own devices, bands played a march or a ragtime tune of their choice once they were a block or so from the cemetery gates. But specific gay numbers were sometimes requested by the burial association or the family.[5] The band's *allegro* departure was customary and inoffensive.

The ceremony of the brass band in a funeral varied, depending on circumstances and requests by the burial association, the church, and the family; but the basic formula was this:[6]

1. The band assembled with members of the burial association at the lodge hall or headquarters. There the procession formed, with the band at the head, lodge standard-bearers next (usually including a furled American flag as well as organizational banners), and lodge members, loosely assembled, behind. A marshall or marshalls headed the band.
2. The band played a hymn at lodge headquarters in dirge tempo, to establish a mood of mourning and solemnity.
3. The procession moved in march tempo to the funeral home, church, or home where the body waited, playing familiar hymns and other pieces as medium-tempo 2/4 marches.
4. At the church the band played an appropriate hymn (chosen by the church or family) in solemn chorale style.
5. The band waited outside the church, usually dis-

persing informally, for the service to conclude. It did not play at this time, so as not to interfere with the preaching and hymn-singing inside. The wait could be very long at an elaborate service.

6. After the service, the band reassembled and played a dirge while the body was carried from the church to the hearse.

7. As the procession reformed and moved with the hearse to the cemetery, the band played dirges and hymns in slow 4/4 dirge tempo.

8. At the cemetery (or at a predetermined point, if the cemetery were too distant for the cortege to walk all the way), the band moved aside, forming the procession into a double rank to create a corridor through which the hearse passed, and the snare drummer played a long roll. This moment, when the band signaled the conclusion of the processional segment of the funeral, was called "turning the body loose."

9. The band might next, according to wishes of the church and family, play a hymn at the graveside, after which the minister might preach again and conduct hymn-singing. A trumpeter from the band might be asked to play "Taps" as a solo.

10. Outside the cemetery, the band regrouped while final rites of interment were performed. The snare drummer tightened his snares (the drum had previously been muffled for dirges and hymns), played a cadence at a bright march tempo, and the band departed.

11. On the return route, once the band had moved a respectful distance from the cemetery, it played marches and popular tunes, either at the leader's discretion or by request. This segment of the procession satisfied second liners and association members accompanying the band, signaled the obsequy's end, and formed a final act of celebration.

12. Back at the lodge hall the band dispersed, to return home or to stop for refreshments inside the hall.

These steps followed traditional etiquette, and any stage might be varied by circumstances. Small symbolic acts attached themselves to the pattern. For instance, jazz tunes on return from the cemetery were popularly supposed to reflect the character of the deceased and his family. Notorious rounders were treated with "Oh, Didn't He Ramble?" or "I'll Be Glad When You're Dead, You Rascal You"; and purportedly naughty widows were admonished with "Lady Be Good." There is doubt about the consciousness of such choices, but the point of the ragtime marches was clear—to break the solemnity of several hours of hymns and dirges and to create a mood of jubilation. The marches might be quasimilitary fare like "Panama," "Bugle Boy March" (adapted from the standard march "The American Soldier"), or "My Maryland"; or they might be ragged versions of hymn tunes used earlier—"Just a Little While to Stay Here," "Sing On,"

"Bye and Bye"; or they could be pop tunes like "Lady Be Good," "You Tell Me Your Dream," or "Down in Honky Tonk Town." Whatever mythology attached to the return parade, it was famous for spontaneous celebration and impromptu community dancing with the street bands.

The funeral procession might vary with the addition of bands—two or more might participate, dividing duties and creating a more complex ceremony. Or there might be various symbolisms and rituals injected into the funeral by fraternal organizations or other societies. The band's role remained that of leading the procession, providing solemn music for marching, and playing religious music en route. The brass band dominated the ceremony emotionally. Its loud, mournful strains carried further in open air and were more persuasive than singing. The military element —muffled snare drum; dull, tolling bass drum in dirges; the wailing quality of wind instruments playing minor-key music—created an impressive, exalted drama, in striking contrast to modern urban funerals at which the corpse is whisked away in sanitized black machinery through back streets, with mourners hidden in limousines, to the privacy of burial. New Orleans funerals were leisurely public acts, theatrical displays designed not to hide burial as a fearful obscenity, but to exhibit it as a community act, the social obligation of friends and family. The brass music with the cortege heralded the procession, published the fact of death and celebrated it.

The music that bands chose or invented for the ceremonies manifests this religious attitude toward death. The common material was church music, usually standard Protestant hymns like "Lead Me Savior," "God Be With You Till We Meet Again," "In the Sweet Bye and Bye," "In the Upper Garden," or spirituals like "Bye and Bye," "Over in the Gloryland," or "Sing On." These were treated in distinct styles for different phases of the ceremony. One might be played first as a march, en route from lodge hall to church, done simply in 2/4 march rhythm. Then it might be played as a slow chorale-like hymn, with the harmonies a church choir would use (basically the four-part soprano/alto/tenor/bass harmony of the hymnals that were generally called "Dr. Watts' Book"). Third, the hymn might be treated as a dirge, either individually or in a medley/potpourri form, at extremely slow 4/4 dirge tempo, played not just in simple harmony, but embellished with solo passages and elaborate variations in the manner of a military dirge.[7]

There is a direct connection between hymn material and dirges. Scored dirges played by the bands, basically nineteenth-century military music, were used alone or in combination with familiar religious music. (See Appendix II herein.) The overt content of the military dirge differs from church music, since the hymns and spirituals were familiar vocal music with texts imprinted in listeners' memories. Strictly instrumental funeral marches, combined with common hymnal material, created a powerful emotional syn-

Eureka Brass Band, *at the graveside, 1951. Left to right: Albert Warner, Emanuel Paul, "Sunny" Henry, Joseph "Red" Clark, Ruben Roddy, Eddie Richardson, Robert Lewis. "I'd rather play a funeral than eat a turkey dinner!"—Willie Pajaud (trumpet with the Eureka Brass Band), in conversation with Richard B. Allen.*

thesis, uniting complex unfamiliar music (the dirges) with materials potent in the community's religious sensibility.

The street bands' style of dirge playing evolved over a century of habit and tradition, and it too was emotionally powerful. The scored dirges require sweet and melancholy brass playing, especially from cornets, trombones, and baritone horns. Most dirges call for careful ensemble work, with fairly complex harmonies and contrapuntal relationships. The tempo is so slow that the rhythmic element is suppressed; and the emphasis is on clearly intoned melody in pronounced *legato* style, with the band becoming almost an *a capella* brass choir. The rhythm is maintained by bass drum, by slow rolls and single beats on the snare drum, and by the bass horn line. Over this is usually woven a dense ensemble melody. Most dirges emphasize a clear middle-range sound—with some high trumpet solos (province of the E^b cornet soloist in old bands); but typical dirges use middle-range solo instruments as much—trombones or baritone horns in lyrical passages more or less equivalent to the tenor vocal range and in heroic tenor style. Playing a dirge well is difficult even for a polished military band, not because the music is exceptionally complex but because it must be played precisely, at an extremely slow tempo, and with every instrument carefully balanced in the ensemble.

Most New Orleans street bands could not reach such perfection. They adopted strategies of style to match the music with the strengths and abilities of their ensemble. The bands dropped, or simplified, passages too complex or ornate for a small band, and they sometimes interpolated hymn melodies into dirges as substitutes for the more esoteric passages. They also produced a looser ensemble sound than a 50-piece military band, since they could not fill out all instrumental parts. Their dirges consequently included pauses or holes in the sound, silences sometimes as effective and eloquent as sound itself. They used an E^b clarinet to achive the high, wailing sound once provided by the rare E^b cornet. They omitted or simplified trumpet and trombone passages to match the music-reading abilities of the musicians. In sum, the dirges, *as played*, were adaptations, not strictly executed stock arrangements.

This made construction of hymn potpourris and homemade dirges simpler. Since most military dirges are simply constructed—two or three brief strains, sometimes only one or two, repeated during route march—it was easy to use a strain from a dirge and a few hymns welded together in medley fashion and played in a uniform dirge style. As in most Afro-American music, the stylistic consistency of the ensemble made the music effective. The blending of instrumental sounds, the contribution of strong solo talents, and the subordination of less-able musicians helped keep dirge-hymn performances simple and eloquent. The heterophonic approach to ensemble playing, characteristic of New Orleans jazz, with all voices taking something near a melodic lead part, made the dirge-hymn sound distinctive and powerful.[8] The collective expression of feeling was more effective because it was homespun, like the singing of a church choir. The wide vibrato, vocal tone coloring, and elliptical attack of the musicians created an inimitable ensemble sound. The brass band, a brass choir with rhythm accompaniment, accentuated the heterophonic qualities of the music, because all instruments excepting the drums could approximate a melodic lead. In dirges and church music, middle-range instruments might dominate melodic passages more than trumpets and clarinet. Thus the bands developed a technique to accommodate a consistent ensemble style as an *additive* process: as many of the eight or ten horns played at once as wished, so that ensemble passages would be dense and complex or solo passages would have one or two horns playing a defined melody over soft ensemble chords.

The brass band displays more root qualities of New Orleans jazz than most jazz ensembles, since the styles of horn players are baldly exposed. No piano or unified string-piano-drums rhythm section masks or ballasts the horns. And each musician is audible, even in ensemble passages. This is one reason that the bands insisted on technical proficiency from members; there is no leeway in a small, tightly knit group for carelessness or uncertainty. Whereas a second clarinetist back in the ranks of a large military band may drop out or misread parts, New Orleans brass bands were pared to minimal essentials, and each musician carried an important part of the load.

Funeral music used by New Orleans street bands was a test for bandsmen. When the bands ceased to function as concert ensembles in parks and as dance bands in halls, scored dirges were the last regularly played written music. Some groups like the Eureka band still played standard marches and vaudeville-circus music into the 1950s, but most abandoned scores except for funeral processions, at which dirge cards were passed out. Simple head arrangements of hymns partially supplanted note-read military dirges. Yet even with the passing of scored music, some of the formality and decorum of earlier bands was retained. Head arrangements of hymns as potpourri-dirges were played in the solemn, crying style of the military arrangements, with muffled drums and unbearably slow cadences. The intonation of the horns was still brassy and plangent, the ritual of the procession still decorous.

It is impossible to recapture the feelings of the funeral procession as bands experienced it, but eyewitness accounts reflect facets of the funeral ceremony and the bands' roles from individual perspectives, describing bands in their milieu, unselfconsciously creating a musical genre over a half-century of experience.

"Taps." *Peter Bocage plays solo trumpet with the Eureka Brass Band, October 10, 1964. "All you had to play was just on that card, you know —if it was a high note, play high notes; if it was a low note, play a low note."–Peter Bocage, William Ransom Hogan Jazz Archive interview, January 29, 1959, p. 52.*

Stereopticon Views on the Road to the Graveyard

The first account is from Warren "Baby" Dodds, one of the most famous and admired New Orleans drummers, who worked with street bands in the years around World War I and rejoined the bands when he returned to the city at the end of World War II. Talking for William Russell about his musical career, Baby Dodds recited the role of the brass band's snare drummer.[9] The recording communicates the poetic quality of Dodds's description, which is in the cadenced, almost strophic, form other musicians have adopted in reminiscences;[10] this excerpt is reproduced as Dodds spoke it, in the form of spontaneous oral verse:

The ordinary brass band
consists of 9 men:
trombone, tuba,
baritone, alto,
sometimes 1 trumpet,
sometimes 2,
E-flat clarinet,
snare drum & bass drum.

You have the cymbal attached
to the top of the bass drum.
And they'll get the cymbal—
this is, they do it with
a man alone, by himself,
beating the cymbal.
And that is his job—
to have both hands going.

And the snare drummer,
well he had work to do.

Cause he had to keep up
with the band
& to play what the band
was playin'.
And then when the band
was stopped he'd have to march—
& that meant he kept the cadence going.
A pretty big job
for 1 man.

I used to do that
for play—
it was fun for me.
And I used to beat the snare drum
& I beat it very loudly.
And the guys could march
by my snare drum just as well
as by the band.

And you wondered
how in the world
a 9-piece brass band
could play the music
those fellows played.
But that's all they had.

Now, about a funeral:
that's the snare drummer's job—
he carries the whole responsibility
on his shoulders,
for the simple reason
that he beats the time
for them to walk.

And he's got to break the time,
cause you don't walk as slow
after you get through playin'
as when you're playin'.

After you're walking
at a certain brisk pace,
you break that down
to a very slow walk,
then the bass drum
gives the last slow beat.
Then you keep that beat
on through the funeral number
that you're playin'.
After you get through with that—
it's very slow—
then the snare drummer's
supposed to pick it up
to a marching time.
Not too fast,
but just fast enough
for a guy not to
burn himself out.

When they put the body
in the ground & say
"ashes to ashes"—
well, that's the drummer's cue
right there,
telling him
to get out of there.
And the snare drummer alone
goes out into the middle
of the street
& he'd start to roll.
And he rolled loud
& you can hear that roll
within a block of where you are
—or I'll say a half a block—
but when you're rolling loud
in the street,

you can hear that drum
on a clear day
for about a block.

And that was my job
to get out & roll
& call the band.
Nobody call the band
but the drummer.
The snare drummer alone.

And you could see guys
jumpin' over graves
& comin' out of people's houses
& out of bar rooms
&, oh, just flyin'.

And it just gave me
so much pleasure to see
those guys that had
overstayed themselves
& come out runnin'.
Some of them
with a sandwich in their hand
or a jelly roll stickin' out
where they're tryin' to chew fast
& get it down.
Some guys with some whiskey
in their hand.
And some guys kiss the woman
& say,
"I'll see you, so long, goodbye"
& the door slam BAM!
see em runnin' down the steps.
Some guys with no cap,
that had left their cap,
had to go back & get it—
their uniform cap.

Oh, it was a lot of fun.
Then they all line up—
line up from the drummer.

Baby Dodds also explained in his memoirs the philosophy of bands in New Orleans funerals:

Of course we played other numbers coming back from funerals. We'd play the same popular numbers that we used to play with dance bands. And the purpose was this: As the family and people went to the graveyard to bury one of their loved ones, we'd play a funeral march. It was pretty sad, and it put a feeling of weeping in their hearts and minds and when they left there we didn't want them to hear that going home. It became a tradition to play jazzy numbers going back to make the relatives and friends cast off their sadness. And the people along the streets used to dance to the music. I used to follow those parades myself, long before I ever thought of becoming a drummer. The jazz played after New Orleans funerals didn't show any lack of respect for the person being buried. It rather showed their people that we wanted them to be happy.[11]

Another witness of the long brass-band tradition, Sunny Henry, stressed the bands' difficult role in the ceremonies and the weight of tradition. He felt, first, that only old, well-organized bands and older bandsmen played the music properly: "They [the hastily constituted "jump-up" bands] don't play no dirge. They might play, sometimes, like—what you call that thing—'Closer Walk with Thee' and something like that, something slow . . . by head. They play 'God Be with Us Till We Meet Again'; well, they play all them things by head, but when you come down to them really dirges, you understand, they can't fool with that, see."[12] Commenting on blues tunes as marches on return from the cemetery, Sunny said, "Sometimes, some of the guys in the parade, they ask for them things, you see, of course what they ask for, we play the blues."[13] He stressed that the march back was not at a breakneck tempo but a comfortable walking pace: "Well, you couldn't play too fast, play in the march tempo. . . . Little faster than the dirge."[14] And he described bandsmen's pay for funeral jobs, drawn from experience over a half-century in New Orleans street bands. At the turn of the century bandsmen were paid $2.00–$2.50 each for a funeral, and by the 1950s they received $6.00 each, with a little more to the leader. Hardly princely wages for a long afternoon's work in all weathers, across miles of city streets or country roads. No wonder bandsmen like Sunny Henry and Willie Pajaud and Peter Bocage played funerals not for the pay or prestige but because they venerated the music and the tradition.

One musician committed to traditions of the bands and the formal music represented by funeral processions was Red Clark, who collected every band score he could find. Clark cataloged the Eureka band's music, urging the band to learn new scores and vary its repertoire. By the late 1950s, the Eureka had drifted far enough from the tradition of strictly read marches and difficult funeral dirges to depress Clark. "Everytime I run across a part of years ago, it gives me the blues."[15] He remembered years when the Eureka

The second line forms *as the band leaves the cemetery. Louis Nelson, with the Olympia Brass Band, October 10, 1964. "That would be the last of the dead man. Everybody would come back home, and they believed truly to stick right to the Bible—that means rejoice at the death and cry at the birth. . . . That was always the end of a perfect death."* — *Jelly Roll Morton, Library of Congress interview (1938).*

band learned new scores and rehearsed them regularly, when the band was famous for its broad repertoire and pleased bystanders with novel scores. He recalled a funeral for the Young and True Friends Benevolent Association, when the Eureka band attracted this compliment: "Well, we'll hear something different today."[16] Musicians like Henry and Clark, perhaps relics of nineteenth-century traditions, kept the bands active, with developing styles and repertoires. The passing of this generation signaled the end of a live brass-band tradition.

Besides musicians themselves, reports exist from onlookers at funeral processions, casual passersby, and interested social historians. Sometimes outside viewpoints show more clearly the impact of the bands in their setting than do the perceptions of the bandsmen who took the music and ceremonies for granted. Richard B. Allen describes the funeral procession for Willie Williams, January 28, 1963, sponsored by the Young and True Friends Benevolent Association and employing the Eureka Brass Band:[17]

En route from church to Carrollton Cemetery, band played "What a Friend We Have in Jesus" and a rather sweet and tuneful dirge, despite the blasting of trombones, which we did not recognize at the time, but were told later had been "Upper Garden." In the cemetery, at the graveside, they played "Just a Closer Walk With Thee" and "God Be With You Till We Meet Again." The Young and True Friends always request that "God Be With You . . ." be played at the funerals of their members, at graveside. During these graveside services, at least one woman "fell out,"

and there was much hubbub over what to do with her—one of her friends insisted that they "roll her over here on the grass, don't put her on that cold concrete, she ain't got no coat on nor nothing." Nobody had any smelling salts, either.

On the way back to the hall, the band played "When the Saints Go Marching In," "St. Louis Blues," "Lord, Lord, Lord," and "Gloryland." They did not go directly back to the hall, but marched out of the Birch Street gate of the cemetery, to Lowerline Street, down Lowerline to Oak, to Fern Street, to Zimpel, back on Zimpel to Burdette and up Burdette to the hall.

"Shanks" was grand marshall out in front of whole procession. Another man, in topcoat, marched beside him, but did not take much of a hand in directing. Another marshall, behind the band and in front of the flag and the "Friends" was "Boo Boo," who Frank Santimore says is the best grand marshall he's ever seen. Shanks maintained some discipline. At the corner of Lowerline and Willow, Shanks halted proceedings because some of the second liners had gotten out into the street in front of the procession. Shanks waved his baton regally and announced, "Get out of the street or we ain't gonna have no music, just gonna walk back." They scampered back up onto the sidewalk. Farther on, an exuberant man in a brown fedora danced out into the street from the lake side—a younger man in light jacket and red cap rushed out from the river side and escorted him back up onto the sidewalk.

As they neared the hall, coming back, Shanks signaled the music to cease rather abruptly. It may have been because the second liners had spilled over into the street again, or because one of the official funeral cars of mourners was in front of the church, pulled out just as the procession came up.

Weather was cold, though sun was out. Crowd not quite so large as sometimes in this area, and dancing not quite so violent, but what there was was good, seemed more spontaneous and less "put-on" than sometimes.

Matthew "Fats" Houston marched with the Young and True Friends, suitably attired. Although he was not marshalling, his manner of walking cannot be anything but a marshall's.

Allen also describes the ceremonies and process of a two-band funeral for Emile Crayton, April 5, 1960, managed by the Zulu Social Aid and Pleasure Club and by the Odd Fellows, employing the Eureka Brass Band and the Young Tuxedo Brass Band. Significant is the musical agenda of the two bands, as they shared duties:

En route to the church—Eureka Brass Band:
  "We Shall Walk Through the Streets of the City"
  "Bye and Bye"
  "Just a Little While to Stay Here"
  "Sing On"
  "When the Saints Go Marching In" (as the funeral procession entered the church)

Approaching church—Young Tuxedo Brass Band:
  "Just a Little While to Stay Here"

From the church to the cemetery—both bands:
  Eureka: "What a Friend We Have in Jesus" (head arrangement)
  Young Tuxedo: "Eternal Peace" (scored dirge)
  Eureka: "#2" (scored dirge)
  Young Tuxedo: "Flee As a Bird to the Mountain" (scored dirge)
  Eureka: "Eternity" (scored dirge)

As the body was "turned loose," trumpeter Andy Anderson of the Young Tuxedo band played "Taps,"

while the other bandsmen stood by and the procession entered the cemetery; this was a variation that sometimes supplanted the drum roll. After the interment, the bands left the cemetery with the two groups managing the funeral and formed two separate processions back to the Zulu Social Aid and Pleasure Club hall and the Odd Fellows hall, dividing up second liners and bystanders between them, following nearly parallel routes across the city.[18] As is evident from the amount of music on this program, a two-band funeral was more splendid and lengthy than smaller ceremonies. We can only imagine the pomp of larger memorial parades with many bands participating and competing.

In the following account, prepared especially for this book, Richard Allen summarizes nearly thirty years of observing New Orleans street bands, offering a composite portrait of a New Orleans funeral procession and its implications:

A New Orleans funeral with a "band of music" is unique each time I experience it. In order to recapture these experiences I shall combine my recollections of many events from many funerals into one story, in order to bring out the pattern and to tell of the men and the customs of New Orleans.

The leading role is played by Ernest Beavers, a porter by trade and a Baptist by faith. He died last week, and his body was held over at the Uptown branch of the Good Citizens Funeral System until his eldest son and daughter could come from California. Mr. Beavers was a member of the Young Men's Olympia Benevolent Association (YMOBA), Senior Division, and the Zulu Social Aid and Pleasure Club.

Forming up *for a Sunday parade and concert—the Young Tuxedo Brass Band, summer, 1974. "The fellows who learn that music don't want to learn; all they want to play is bebop. Don't want to learn that lead on a 6/8 march, don't want to play that. Got to learn them 6/8."* —John Casimir, William Ransom Hogan Jazz Archive interview, January 17, 1958, p. 40.

Both organizations are social in nature, but they also have death benefits that serve as life insurance. A member can have a brass band for his funeral if he wishes—and if his widow does not go against his request. Some widows believe the use of these brass bands is wrong; some need money; some want the money. At this time, a chilly day just before Christmas, a brass band of ten men charges about seventy dollars for such a job, and the widow has hired the Eureka and the Young Tuxedo.

The Young Men, many of whom look to be at least sixty, and the Eureka meet at the Old Bulls Club, now an Elks Hall, on Eighth near Daneel Street. The time for the procession is set at 11:30 A.M., to allow for inevitable latecomers.

The Zulus and the Young Tuxedo are meeting at Pete's Blue Heaven, a bar on South Rampart Street. Just as they start off, a young, dark cornetist runs up, panting; but in a minute or two he manages to blow their theme, "Lord, Lord, Lord, You Sure Been Good to Me," with vigor. I find out later, outside the church, that he had played all night with a modern jazz combo on Bourbon Street and has thus overslept. His few hours of rest are broken into because he has not had the pleasure of playing a funeral for so long. He has enjoyed some fame for his solo part on a recording of a rock-and-roll tune based on "Just a Closer Walk with Thee."

The second line is mostly neighborhood youths with a few grey heads thrown in. There is almost no dancing at first, and the band seems to be waiting for this inspiration. After a march to snare drum alone, the band surprises everybody with "Jingle Bells," and the Christmas spirits begin to flow from half-pint bottles of whiskey and fifths of muscatel and sweet vino. The dancing gets hotter and there are more dancers. After this, the band strikes up "Over in the Gloryland," softening down at the approach to the Israel Baptist Church. The Zulus enter the church. Some second liners wait at the church. Since the town is full of people known as "street ramblers," the second line grows as the procession goes along.

About 12:30 P.M., the Eureka and the YMOBA leave the hall to "Just a Little While to Stay Here," their theme. The second line here is even more sedate, as the society is more "classified," that is, higher class, than are the members of a pleasure club like the Zulus. The followers remain on the sidewalk. Again, they are mostly young men; but there are also a few English musicians, some Tulane graduate students, and three workers from the Archives of New Orleans Jazz. The Eureka attracts these people because its sound is more traditional than that of the Young Tuxedo. There is more dignity to the bearing of this organization, and the Eureka knows that it should play only hymns. Percy Humphrey sounds a few bars of "Sweet Fields" to announce his hymn choice and the key in which it is to be played. The band turns onto Jackson Avenue and, as it nears the church, plays quietly but with intensity. Some of the members of the Young Tuxedo stare resentfully at the rival group. The Young Men go into the church, joining the congregation and the Zulus, and another wait begins. The dead man was a good member of this church, and the regular minister as well as three invited ministers, including one Reverend Harang [!], will preach. The service is going on, and the musicians tell me it will probably last two more hours.

The sun is warming up the downtown side of the street, and some of the second line and band members are sitting on the box steps of nearby houses. Most of us head for the nearest bar as soon as the hymn is over. In the dark, narrow, noisy room Paul Barnes, the alto saxophonist, talks about a funeral with eleven preachers, each one trying to outdo the others in his sermon; when that procession finally arrived at the graveyard, it had closed and the body had to remain unburied until the next day.

Albert Warner and Sunny Henry order a half-pint of gin.

Their friendship is as tight as their teamwork on the trombones. Sunny jokes with Albert about losing money on the last funeral, accusing him of being a hog. Albert had spent a lot, drinking in his carefully measured way, finishing the last drink in the last half-pint just as the service finished, not at all like a hog. We talk about who first played the clarinet solo in "High Society," boxing, gamblers, and the day Eddie Jackson blew down a fence with his tuba. Suddenly Percy Humphrey walks in, announcing, "Heads up, gentlemen." The musicians obey orders, straightening up, throwing back their heads, throwing down their drinks.

Outside, the Eureka changes to dirge tempo with "In the Upper Garden," while the congregation sings "In the Sweet Bye and Bye." The church bell sounds, and the body is brought out. Robert "Son Fewclothes" Lewis, the Eureka bass drummer, holds the time strictly, despite distractions. We move toward Lafayette Cemetery Number Two, with the Young Men and the Eureka leading. Next the Young Tuxedo plays "Eternal Peace," a funeral march. A woman screams, "That music, that music tears me up!" A friend leads her away; both are sobbing. John Casimir's E-flat clarinet keeps up the piercing wails. Challenged, Percy Humphrey reaches in a cloth sack hung over his shoulder and pulls out the music of "51." This is what the New Orleans musicians call heavy music, a type that is hard for many musicians to read but that plumbs deep. Henry and Warner's trombones now have the melody, playing it with majesty. The members of this band are all sure of their ability, and their sureness shows.

Both organizations and bands break ranks at the graveyard gate and straggle to the Young Men's tomb. There is a short service, interrupted briefly by the seeming impossibility of getting the large coffin into the ovenlike opening. The Eureka band plays "What a Friend We Have in Jesus."

After the burial the bands and organizations assemble on Washington Avenue. The second line's nerves seem to tighten up, until there is a roll on the snare drum and three booming beats on the bass drum, signaling a new tempo and a new spirit. The mood of the music hits you, and your feelings are turned upside down. A spontaneous yell of pure joy pushes the wailing to the back of your mind, and the shaking starts with "When the Saints Go Marching In," by the Young Tuxedo. The procession splits in half, heading back to the starting points. The Eureka and the Young Men are loosening up with "Victory Walk," an old tune that must be one of the ancestors of rock-and-roll. The solemnity of the organization is put aside for a swaggering strut. The officers keep the second line out of the street, in spite of the barrelhouse excitement of the Eureka. They start a favorite piece, "Lady Be Good." This is often played coming back from the graveyard—as a reminder to the widow. Several young "studs" begin to circle around an umbrella that has been dropped in the street. The grand marshall motions them out of the way of the procession. They move back to the sidewalk when he yells, "No more music." If he stops the band, it will break their hearts. By now the hall is just around the corner, but the grand marshall takes the long way home, going a couple of blocks further uptown. He makes a left turn and the band goes into "Panama." After a block he makes another left turn. The trombones stick out of the ensemble with a sliding chorus that Sunny and Albert have worked out. The umbrellas rise and fall like a wave as the procession nears the Old Bulls' Hall. As Percy Humphrey's trumpet rises above the mass of sound, the Young Men head into the hall.

Meanwhile the Young Tuxedo has moved on toward its starting point. When the band hits Rampart Street, a woman who cried, "My cousin, O my little cousin!" all the way to the graveyard suddenly decides to shake down every building they pass on the way to Pete's Blue Heaven.

Brass-band veterans *with the Eureka Brass Band, 1956. Left to right: Emanuel Paul, John Casimir, Alphonse Picou, Albert Warner, "Sunny" Henry.*

The second line likes blues, and they get plenty of them returning to the bar. John Casimir's "Whoopin' Blues" raises shouts, jugs of wine, and umbrellas. The band followers yell their lungs out each time a brief space in the music opens up. This must be the only tune that ends abruptly with two bars of silence on the part of every instrument in the band. After a last shout, the second liners moan in disappointment at the mean trick of cutting off the music with no ending. The band drops out for their whooping break and does not start up again. The Young Tuxedo switches to an unusual mixture with "Perdido."

The trumpets sound strange to me with their modern riffs against the old-time squeals of Casimir's clarinet. The contrast does not worry the second liners, who are now shaking with a frenzy. A circle forms around two of the dancers who are showing their stuff. A grand marshall "makes his turn" unexpectedly, and the second line is swept along on the beat without noticing that the procession has sneaked away around the corner. The second liners run to catch up, and a block later the Young Tuxedo and the Zulus march into Pete's Blue Heaven. The bar is soon too packed for us to get inside. The music stops, and it is all over.

It is possible to speculate that these funerals fill some unconscious need or what have you, caused by ghost fears or ancestor worship. But I prefer to think that the dead man wanted to "die as he lived," to quote an old New Orleans saying. According to Horace White, a locally known second liner, his friends came to honor him "because why? We loved you, and . . . you . . . always like music, so we give you music."

Another view of the funeral proceedings, valuable as the perspective of a visitor, is by jazz journalist Whitney Balliett, who surveyed the New Orleans jazz scene in 1965 in an essay entitled "Mecca, La." His description of a country funeral attended by the Olympia Brass Band and the Young Tuxedo Brass Band conveys vividly the sights and sounds of the procession from church to cemetery:[19]

The church door opened, and two women in black and white, their faces wet and contorted, hobbled out on the arms of several men. A file of men wearing Odd Fellows' ceremonial aprons and neckpieces followed. The Young Tuxedo Band and the Olympia Band played a slow "Just a Closer Walk with Thee." Then the Olympia marched past the church and turned into Ames Boulevard, with the Young Tuxedo about fifty feet behind. A dozen Odd Fellows walked between them. The snare drum was muffled and the beat as slow as Big Ben's. "Savior Lead Me," by the Olympia, was followed by the Young Tuxedo's "What a Friend We Have in Jesus." Dead, soft drumbeats separated the numbers. The second line ambled along quietly at one side of the road, and a long string of limousines nosed the Young Tuxedo. The procession moved between a housing development and a farmyard full of charging guinea hens, between a power station and a field of cows, and after a mile or so it halted at a wooden bridge over a deep ditch. On the other side, a dirt road disappeared into a patch of woods. The Young Tuxedo marched across the bridge, followed by the hearse, which moved cautiously, filling the bridge. The cemetery began on the left of the dirt road, and was a bedraggled sea of small stones, briars, wooden crosses, and long grass. Refuse had been dumped as fill on the other side of the road. A tunnel of trees dripped and whispered. The Young Tuxedo played "Savior Lead Me" at the grave, and after the service the mourners walked slowly back to the boulevard. The Young Tuxedo suddenly started "When the Saints Go Marching In." The second line materialized in front. The music was thin and loose, compared with the New Orleans parade, and twice as brave. The sun came out, burnishing one of the tubas. The Olympia began a fast "Just a Closer Walk with Thee." In the second line, a fat man dressed in a tight blue suit and a small fedora threw back his head, switched his hips, and strutted through a crowd of leaping, delighted children. The two tear-drenched women from the church danced arm in arm. An old woman flopped heavily in circles, like a turkey with an injured wing, and was joined by an old man, who pumped his knees and trembled his hands. The returning limousines roared past, leaving big white dust devils. The Young Tuxedo played "Bye and Bye." The road was filled with dancers, and when the rain started again there were little screams. I looked down, and half a dozen tiny pistonlike children were sharing my umbrella. Their turned-up faces were split by smiles, and their cheeks were covered with rain.

We moved into Third Street and stopped in front of the house belonging to the head of the Odd Fellows. The old woman danced into a front yard across the street and onto the porch. Both bands, packed into a circle, played "Lord, Lord, Lord." It was a glorious five minutes. Twenty instruments rose and fell in broken, successive waves. The rain let up, and the music ended, stunning us all. The dancers ran down, and I could hear cars on Ames Boulevard. A thin middle-aged man in a cowboy hat came up to me. "That was my papa was buried today," he said, smiling. "Fifty years he was an Odd Fellow."

This account captures the sorrow and joy mingled in these funeral processions, as well as the feeling of parody sometimes created by the second line in its strutting and dancing, its satire of military (and social) pomp and splendor. It also pictures the bands inside their milieu, for up-country funerals were often worked by New Orleans bands, since the city is closely ringed by hamlets, plantations, and lakeside villages.

These views may give a mosaic impression of a funeral procession from inside and out. They cannot convey nuances of feeling in the music itself. The combination of the ritualistic procession, the musical offerings of the band, and the somber attention of the mourners is a complex theatrical event, a mixed-media vernacular drama generated by community feelings and beliefs. More than a folk-art form, it is a liturgical expression accompanied by traditional elements. We cannot preserve this ritual, as we have preserved offices of the Catholic church in masses by Palestrina and Bach. But the black funeral procession has been a strong artistic and religious expression, valuable because it was created by people denied other means of developing art and culture. Like the spirituals, jubilees, and folk-hymns of the middle nineteenth century, the music of these New Orleans funeral ceremonies is a powerful expression of black vernacular culture in America.

Aside from the ritual duties of the funerals, New Orleans street bands fulfilled many functions, social and musical. Their place in the community is worth review. Brass bands enjoyed great popularity through the first two decades of the twentieth century, even while dance bands and small wind-string ensembles playing popular music were strong rivals. Eventually street bands lost some of their social functions and became increasingly specialized, playing almost solely as marching units for parades and ceremonies. By the end of the 1920s, when the Depression closed down much of the popular entertainment industry in New Orleans, as elsewhere, the oldest generation of bandsmen had retired or died. After the Depression most old-line bands had dissolved as standing organizations, though many bandsmen were still active. When bands reorganized at the end of World War I, many changes occurred. The most basic change was the loss of middle-range brass—alto and baritone horns. These instruments were almost entirely supplanted by alto and tenor saxophones, often playing the same parts but nevertheless injecting a dance-band element into the band's sound.

By the late 1950s much brass-band work was a self-conscious revival effort. Bandsmen and entrepreneurs made the street bands symbolic of jazz history and tradition, and their work was moved still further from the neighborhood-community level at which it had begun. They became showpieces more than grass-roots musical organizations actively connected with social and fraternal movements. This tendency accelerated through the 1960s, as more veteran brass bandsmen died or retired; the tradition itself has now almost disappeared.

Questions remain about the history of the movement. One problem is the development of instrumental roles in New Orleans brass bands and the relationship of these roles to jazz. The brass-band tradition encompasses two streams of development—the straight reading tradition inherited from nineteenth-century bands and their schools of legitimate musicians, and the turn-of-the-century ragtime tradition of musicians who relied on "ear" practices and ingenious head arrangements more than on printed scores. The comingling of these strains in New Orleans music is important to the history of jazz. We can trace it in the careers of influential individual musicians and we can see it in general trends.

For an example of the more general influences, we might look at the saxophone and its role in the brass bands, which parallels that instrument's role in New Orleans jazz. One "fact" older musicians reiterate in interviews is that no one in New Orleans played the saxophone in popular music for years after the turn of the century.[20] The prominent brass-band tradition, emphasizing military-band instrumentation, influenced this. Clarinets and flutes were acceptable reeds for bands, but the middle range of ensembles, brass band or dance band, was filled by brass or string instruments. Later, reed players doubled from clarinet to various saxes, but the process was slow. It occurred in the 1920s and probably owed more to influences from outside the city than to native practices. Beginning about 1920, popular dance bands recorded in the North featured saxophone work. Even more influential were vaudeville "novelty" and pit-band routines, such as those of Rudy Wiedoft or the widely traveled Six Brown Brothers act, featuring an all-

Nightingale Social Aid and Helping Hand Club, *on parade in 1952,
headed by a "splendid brass band." "I'll be perfectly honest with you—
I have never seen such beautiful clubs as they had in the city of New
Orleans."—Jelly Roll Morton, Library of Congress interview (1938).*

saxophone ensemble playing tricky arrangements of popular tunes. This latter group advertised instruments and instrumental method courses—a promotional vehicle for saxophone manufacturers. The rococo sound of such novelty routines partially accounts for the dominant saxophone style featured in dance bands of the early and middle 1920s—Fletcher Henderson's early bands and popular white groups like Paul Whiteman's, the Coon-Sanders Nighthawks, and the Jean Goldkette bands.

As these "modern" trends reached New Orleans, musicians adopted them. Most clarinet players learned to double on saxophone. New Orleans bands like the Original Tuxedo Jazz Orchestra, the Jones-Collins Astoria Hot Eight, Piron's New Orleans Orchestra, and Sam Morgan's Jazz Band, recorded during the middle and late 1920s, reflect this influence. It is hardly accidental that the saxophone became for middle America the super-symbol of the "Jazz Age,"an instrument as attractive to youth of the era as the electric guitar was to the youngster of 1965. College dance bands and amateur jazz groups were dominated by saxophonists only barely in control of their instruments, as a sampling of any mediocre dance-band records of the day demonstrates. In the hands of creative musicians the saxophone was absorbed into New Orleans bands. Gradually the availability of saxophonists from dance band work made the instruments adaptable to brass bands, replacing the alto and baritone horns that had become increasingly specialized as brass bands became less popular. This shift in instrumentation affected the basic style and repertoire of street bands.

The influence of individual musicians is epitomized in a few careers. The dominant figures in the early tradition were cornetists, generally leaders of brass bands who were central to the nineteenth-century idea of the "silver cornet band." If saxophonists were popular idols in the 1920s, the heroic figures of earlier bands were cornet virtuosi. These musicians represented an American tradition that went back to the first great keyed-bugle artists of the 1840s and their demonstrations of triple-tonguing and lightning fingering. A provincial bandmaster was presumed to be an accomplished cornet soloist who could conduct the band with one hand while reeling off *presto* triple-tongued variations on "The Carnival of Venice."

Some cornetists in New Orleans bands at the turn of the century illustrate this virtuosity. The disciplined technician and agile sight-reader, a strict "musicianer" in New Orleans argot, was widely respected. Examples were Manuel Perez of the Onward Brass Band, Arnold Metoyer, Papa Celestin of the Tuxedo Brass Band, Peter Bocage, Louis Dumaine, arranger for the WPA concert band, and many others. These men were able players who could follow scores, had polished instrumental attack and tone, and could command a band with their solo work. But they were also recognized to be limited because they were straight players who could not "get off" on tunes, could not improvise or invent hot solos. Schooled as brass bandsmen, most were limited to *embellishing* figures rather than creating true variations. They tended to play the lead melody correctly, as written, without adding syncopations or varying the attack significantly from the on-beat.

The practice for many of these musicians, as they understood the popularity of the new ragtime music and saw improvising musicians received well on the streets, was to accede to public demand and employ improvising musicians. Thus Manuel Perez took Joe Oliver into the Onward Brass Band,[21] Papa Celestin took Louis Armstrong into the Tuxedo Brass Band (and included a hot second cornet in his dance orchestras). It became common practice to divide trumpet chores between hot men and straight readers. The broadened repertoires demanded this solution; otherwise, bands would have been forced to specialize their music. Some friction occurred in this dichotomy between "legitimate" and hot music and musicians. Some players, like Bunk Johnson, spanned both musics comfortably, but others never did and most preferred one music over the other.

Similar division applied to dance bands, which had to supply current popular music read from stock arrangements and another fund of head music improvised on the spot. Some reading musicians solved the problem by widening their repertoire of stock arrangements and drilling players in score-reading. John Robichaux prided himself on having *all* the latest popular songs in stock arrangements for his orchestra as soon as they became available, and he kept a satchel full of new music on the bandstand, ready to supply any request—from scores. Other bandsmen, less skilled in reading, became adept at "faking," as the process was aptly called—playing quick ear arrangements of tunes, not always accurately but with bravado. Many New Orleans musicians fell between these extremes—they "spelled" a bit even if they could not read music well, could play stock arrangements with some prompting, could fake adroitly enough to play pop tunes.

The practice of using two cornets in early New Orleans jazz groups relates to this division of lead chores between hot and straight men. All bets were covered with one good reader and one good faker. Many noted hot-trumpet men—Buddy Petit, Chris Kelly, Freddie Keppard—were not especially associated with brass bands in the 1920s. They are remembered for blues playing with jazz groups, the special province of the "faker" as long as legitimate men like Manuel Perez and Arnold Metoyer dominated street bands. Reading musicians made some forays into jazz and dance work, but only a few (Peter Bocage with A. J. Piron's New Orleans Orchestra, for instance) prospered outside reading street bands. Papa Celestin, for one example, succeeded more as an entrepreneur and showman than as a hot-trumpet star. Other outlets were available, however: Bunk Johnson jobbed for years with circuses, medicine shows, minstrel troupes, and traveling vaudeville bands, as did Punch Miller,[22] Arnold Metoyer, and other New Orleans trumpeters. This was a circular process—since many earlier brass bandsmen of New Orleans had apprenticed with these shows, and the circus-vaudeville tradition, with its *presto* galops, trombone rags, and novelty music, had helped develop New Orleans street bands at the end of the nineteenth century.

The influence of brass bands on jazz in the 1920s is vividly depicted in the careers of Joe Oliver and Louis Armstrong, two great improvising trumpet virtuosi who learned music-reading and technical abc's from brass bandsmen. Both men went North, succeeded as bandleaders and solo stars, and personified jazz for most people. Oliver's career from 1923 to 1928 is one of unbroken triumphs in the cruelly competitive world of big-time northern show business, an environment starkly different from the relaxed, casual world of New Orleans music-making. Oliver introduced Louis Armstrong into the same milieu, and his triumphs overshadowed Oliver's own. A brilliant musical director, Oliver pioneered in creating a tightly unified jazz group and selling it as popular entertainment. Armstrong was less the bandleader and more the virtuoso soloist, like the nineteenth-century silver cornet maestro. He grew as a comedian, singer, and monumental personality in entertainment, but when he came to Chicago as Joe Oliver's second cornet he was straight from the old brass-band days in New Orleans.

Influences are also clear in the tradition of New Orleans reed (clarinet) playing. The city's great reed teachers, the Baquet and Tio families, were strict reading musicians with brass bands and "sit-down" orchestras. These men taught the great New Orleans clarinetists—Jimmie Noone, Omer Simeon, Barney Bigard—and their influence was universal. They fostered the clear, large tone and clean attack that marked great early jazz clarinetists, a limpidity and grace distinguishing New Orleans reedmen from those in the North and East. The Tios' Mexican heritage added the precision of Spanish band practices to the New Orleans style.

The same observations apply to New Orleans drumming, basically a rudimental system from military traditions. The first generation of New Orleans jazz drummers studied under bandsmen like "Old Man" Louis Cottrell, Sr., and Dave Perkins (who played with Jack Laine's white brass bands and taught drums and brass to black and white musicians in the first decade of the century). These men taught rudimental drumming (the traditional "drum-call" military method that teaches technique through a series of rhythmic figures elaborated in an additive process). A pupil who learned the rudiments could read the relatively simple percussion parts for marches and stock orchestrations. The system built from the press roll— the flam/ruff, strokes by which a drummer creates a roll of varying length and density. Drummers like Warren "Baby" Dodds, Zutty Singleton, "Monk" Hazel, Andrew Hilaire, Tony Sbarbaro, and Minor "Ram"

Recording the Eureka Brass Band. *The first recording session for a permanently organized New Orleans brass band, August, 1951. Musicians, left to right: Ruben Roddy, George Lewis, Emanuel Paul, Arthur Ogle, Robert "Son Fewclothes" Lewis, Joseph "Red" Clark, Percy Humphrey, Albert Warner, Eddie Richardson, "Sunny" Henry, Willie Pajaud. "After [George Moret] died, then I took the leadership, see, of the Excelsior Brass Band. Well, then, we played a lot of marches, too, and we used to mix up a little jazz in there, see? But now the brass bands of today, practically most—it seems like the public wants it, and that's what they're giving them is mostly all jazz, you see?—outside of funeral marches, you know." —Peter Bocage, William Ransom Hogan Jazz Archive interview, January 29, 1959, p. 52.*

Hall exemplify the rudimental style applied to jazz. The role of bass drummers in street bands differed from that of snare drummers, however; and the bass drummers were specialists. Their influence was not just on other drummers but on whole bands, because their ability to invent new bass drum beats and to swing an entire brass band in a syncopating manner was more than just a drum style. It was an approach to basic rhythm; just as a strong bass player controls rhythmic patterns in a jazz band, the bass drummer at once anchored and steered his band. Great bass drummers like "Black Benny" Williams, Clay Jiles, Jack Laine, and Robert "Fewclothes" Lewis are remembered as special musicians outside instrumental categories.

Other instrumental traditions descend directly from the brass band: the "tailgate" trombone style, with its circus-band smears, military tone, and punching counterpoint accents, is a step off the street. Percussive string bass styles of George "Pops" Foster, Steve Brown, Alcide "Slow Drag" Pavageau, and the legion of great bassists derive from the brass band less directly, but the basic rhythmic influence is there. The punchy "slapping" style and driving 4/4 pattern of jazz bassists derives from playing with rough, loud brass musicians who demanded a strong percussive bass foundation—almost like the bass drum patterns of the street band.

Aside from influencing instrumental techniques and styles, brass bands also broadened and enriched the repertoires of musicians and groups. When a tune like "High Society" became a local favorite, it was played by brass bands and every vernacular ensemble,[23] as well as by soloists like Storyville piano professors who had to reproduce popular requests. When Jelly Roll Morton sought an example to demonstrate his conception of "New Orleans style," he picked "Panama," the brass-band evergreen, and played a magnificent piano version of the jazz march.[24] This was a reciprocal process, as piano rags were played by bands and orchestras and dance music was adapted (see "Panama" itself) as marches.

But the bedrock of the New Orleans jazz repertoire remained street music—marches and religious music played in brass-band fashion. In the jazz revival of the 1940s much music recorded by bands like Bunk Johnson's, Kid Ory's, Papa Celestin's, or George Lewis' came from the brass-band stockpile. Titles like "High Society," "Panama," "1919 Rag," "My Maryland," "Bugle-Boy March" occur repeatedly. The style of this generation of jazzmen—those growing up with Kid Ory, Louis Armstrong, the Dodds brothers—was formed around 1910–1915. Martial and sentimental music of the Great War mixed with older band music: "Over There," "It's a Long Way to Tipperary," "Bless Them All," "When I Leave This World Behind," "Smiles." This was perhaps the last fresh infusion of military music into the New Orleans tradition.[25] In the 1890s, with the impact of ragtime and cakewalk music in the cities, the Salvation Army created a little march-hymn with a distinct cakewalk rhythm—"Throw Out the Lifeline"—for its brass-vocal choirs. Thus their streetcorner bands competed with saloon nickelodeons and followed Luther's injunction to steal the good tunes back from the devil. The amalgamation of march rhythms, syncopation, and religious texts appears again in New Orleans street bands' renditions of "We Shall Walk Through the Streets of the City," "Lily of the Valley," and similarly adaptable hymns.

Changes in martial and religious music by street bands emphasized the music's joyful and mobile elements. A New Orleans parade is a vigorous exercise in eurhythmics, in dance, as much as an opportunity for drill-team swagger. The music compels the bystander to move and dance; there are no passive spectators at a New Orleans parade. Even at its most somber—in the melancholy dirges—the music stirs. Ghosts of waltzes and schottisches and quadrilles, of nineteenth-century triple-meter dances, haunt slow solo passages in dirges like "Garlands of Flowers" or "West Lawn Dirge." The lyricism of these funeral chants is not only vocal, in the best French manner, but balletic also.

The hybridization of four-square American military marches with Afro-American impulses to displace beats and shift accents is an explanation for the genesis of jazz. The process changed the plodding, walking march measure into a varied dance rhythm. The march beat shifted from the stiff 1-and-3 accent of military cadence to the springy 2-and-4 of Afro-American music—syncopations entered. This musical process, absorbed and altered by Midwestern piano ticklers, emerged as ragtime; then ragtime reentered the brass band in the 1890s with the folk syncopations regularized, conventionalized, and notated. Once marching bands reabsorbed the ragtime feeling, there was no returning to the old straight-ahead playing. Everything emerged with swing, with subtle syncopation.

Perhaps the most profound effects of the street bands came from the love of display, socializing, and celebration in the New Orleans character. The brass bands were ideal for the social clubs, because they permitted a bit of strutting through the streets, a bit of dancing, ballyhoo when needed, soft music for picnics, the uniquely solemn/joyous notes of departure for funerals. The brass-band tradition in America encouraged military charades, also—uniforms, medallions, epaulets, the esoteric ritual of drills and parading, a feeling of patriotism, local pride, self-esteem as a uniformed, polished, proper member of American society.

The combination of ceremonial display and Afro-American swing made a New Orleans parade a stirring drama. Caricature of white folks' pomposity and subtler self-parody made the ritual intriguing. This ingrained humor, which also created masters of vaudeville like Bert Williams, is perhaps the saving grace of the black vernacular musico-theatrical tradition. The comedy appeared in King Zulu parades during Mardi Gras, traditionally elaborate parodies of the Mardi Gras parade paraphernalia: instead of King Rex with his quasidignified exaltation rode King Zulu, dispensing not coins and gewgaws but coconuts hurled like cannonballs into the mob. This anti-masque was black New Orleans' response to the charades of white society.[26] Comedy pervaded New Orleans parade music and rituals without destroying their serious purposes. And this self-aware comedy and dignity created the deepest feelings of the music. Evocations like Paul Barbarin's "Bourbon Street Parade" or "The Second Line" or the Bob Crosby band's "South Rampart Street Parade" depict traditional parades without actually quoting from older marches. When New Orleans jazz is condescendingly referred to as mere "good-time" music, a witless compliment has been paid to the humor and vitality of the parade tradition.

The roots of New Orleans jazz tap the brass-band tradition, and the immense impact of jazz on American popular culture is obvious. After 1920 white America scrubbed away the burnt cork of its blackface parodies and became blacker inside—achieved some degree of "soul," willing or not. And one voice in the Afro-American diapason was the brass music of New Orleans. As their functions and traditions in the city withered, their music was carried around the world by young men who had followed the old bands. In New Orleans today, looking down old streets in an old city, there is a sense of expectation, a feeling that at any moment a small band in bright new uniforms might step around that distant corner, with the sound reaching you, a sound as lost and present as a train whistle in the night.

Appendix I **Materials for Further Study**

A Roster of Brass Bands

The following bands are those for whom some documentation exists, and the lists of personnel are collective catalogs of musicians associated with the bands over a period of years. The listings are not wholly complete, but they reflect research into the backgrounds of New Orleans musicians by several workers, notably Samuel B. Charters, Al Rose, and Edmond Souchon. Dates for the existence of bands are often wholly approximate.

The following abbreviations for musical instruments are given in parentheses after the names of the musicians cited below:

b.d. bass drum
b.h. bass horn (tuba or Sousaphone)
clt. clarinet
d. drum
s.d. snare drum
tbn. trombone
tpt. trumpet (or cornet)

Allen Brass Band (*ca.* 1907–1950)—10 pieces: Henry Allen, Sr. (leader), Peter Bocage, Joe Howard, Oscar Celestin (tpts.), Jack Carey, Buddy Johnson, Yank Johnson, Harrison Barnes (tbns.); Lawrence Duhe (clt.); Wallace Collins (baritone horn); James A. Palao (alto horn); Bebé Matthews (s.d.); Clay Jiles, Red Allen (b.d.)

Bulls Club Brass Band (*ca.* 1915–1925)—10 pieces: Manuel Calier (leader), Joe Oliver, George McCullum, Sr. (tpts.); Arthur Stevens (tbn.).

Camelia Brass Band (1917–1923)—10 pieces: Wooden Joe Nicholas (leader), Buddy Petit (tpts.); Ike Robinson, Joseph Petit, Eddie Morris (tbns.); Alphonse Picou, Johnny Brown (clt.); Buddy Lack (b.h.); Arthur Ogle (s.d.); Henry "Booker T" Glass (b.d.).

Columbia Brass Band (1897–1900)—10–12 pieces: Alcibiades Jeanjacques, Punkie Valentin (tpts.); Bouboul Valentin (tbn.); Alphonse Picou (clt.); Edward Boisseau (baritone horn); Isidore Barbarin (alto horn); Dee Dee Chandler (b.d.).

Diamond Stone Brass Band (*ca.* 1897)—10–12 pieces: Edward Clem (tpt.), Frank Jackson (b.d.).

Eclipse Brass Band (1900–1917): Magnolia Plantation Band—James Humphrey (leader, tpt.); Chris Kelly, Sam Morgan (tpts.); Sunny Henry, Harrison Barnes (tbns.).

Eureka Brass Band (1920–)—10 pieces: Willie Wilson (first leader), Tom Albert, Alcide Landry, "Kid Shots" Madison, Dominique "T-Boy" Remy (second leader), Willie Pajaud, Eddie Richardson, Percy Humphrey (third leader), "Kid Shiek" Colar, Peter Bocage, Willie Weber, ——— Zeno (tpts.); Willie Cornish, Jim Robinson, Earl Humphrey, Albert Warner, Eddie Summers, Louis Nelson, Sunny Henry, Oscar "Chicken" Henry, Joe Avery, —— Shepherd, —— Mullin (tbns.); George Lewis, Albert Burbank, Willie Humphrey (clts.); Alphonse Johnson, Buddy Alphonse (alto horns); Johnny Wilson (baritone horn); Ruben Roddy (alto sax); "Tats" Alexander, Emanuel Paul (tenor saxes); Joseph "Red" Clark, Wilbert Tillman (b.h.); Arthur Ogle, Alfred Williams, CiE Frazier (s.d.); "Black Happy" Goldston, Willie Parker, Robert Lewis (b.d.).

Excelsior Brass Band (1880–1931)—10–12 pieces: Theogene Baquet (first leader, 1880–1904); George Moret (second leader, 1904–1920); Peter Bocage (third leader, 1920–1931); Edward Clem, Frank Jackson, Fice Quiere, James McNeil, James Williams, George Hooker, Arnold Metoyer, Nelson Jean, Paul Thomas, Adolphe Alexander, Sr., Hypolite Charles, Sidney Desvigne, George McCullum, Sr. (tpts.); Aaron Clark, Anthony Page, Harrison Barnes, Baptiste Deslisle, Honore Dutrey, Barnard Raphael, Buddy Johnson, Eddie Vinson, Sunny Henry (tbns.); George Baquet, Alphonse Picou, Lorenzo Tio, Sr., Lorenzo Tio, Jr., Luis Tio, Charles McCurdy, Sam Dutrey, Sr., Willie Humphrey (clts.); Hackett Bros., Joe Payen, Isidore Barbarin, Ralph Montegue (alto horns); Edward Boisseau, Vic Gaspard, George Hooker (baritone horns); Frank Jackson, Frank Robinson (b.h.); Louis Cottrell, Sr., Dee Dee Chandler (s.d.); John Robichaux, Clay Jiles (b.d.).

Fischer's Brass Band (ca. 1915): George Barth, Harry Shannon, Richard Brunies, Manuel Mello (tpts.); Leonce Mello, Cack Riley, "Happy" Schilling, Henry Brunies, Merritt Brunies (tbns.); Johnny Fischer (leader, clt.); Tony Shannon (baritone horn); Freddy Williams, Arthur "Monk" Hazel (d.).

E. Gibson Brass Band (ca. 1945–1965)—9 pieces: Eddie Richardson, Johnny Wimberley, Leon Bajeon, John Henry McNeil (tpts.); Carroll "Cal" Blunt, F. Thompson, Eddie Morris, Eddie Noble (tbns.); Robert Davis (alto sax); A. B. Spears (manager, tenor sax); Louis Keppard, Albert Miller (b.h.); George Sterling (s.d.); Dave Bailey (b.d.).

Holmes Band of Lutcher (ca. 1910): Professor Anthony Holmes (leader, tpt.); Joe Porter (tpt.); Dennis Harris (clt.); "Papa John" Joseph (sax); John Porter (baritone horn); David Jones (alto horn, s.d., and sax); Floyd Jackson (b.h.); Nub Jacobs (b.d.).

Kid Howard's Brass Band (ca. 1945–1950)—10 pieces: Avery "Kid" Howard (leader, tpt.); Alvin Fernandez (tpt.); Jim Robinson (tbn.); Edward Johnson, Ernest Poree, Andrew Morgan (saxes); William Brown (b.h.); James Wilson (s.d.); George Williams (b.d.).

Lions Brass Band (ca. 1928)—10 pieces: Pop Hamilton (leader); Alcide Landry, Manuel Trapp (tpts.); Maurice French, Tom Steptoe (tbns.); Willie Parker (clt.); Lumis Hamilton (French horn); "Shiek-O" (baritone horn); Ernest Rogers (s.d.); Arthur Turner (b.d.).

Melrose Brass Band (ca. 1900–1910)—10 pieces: Joe Oliver, Adam Olivier, Bunk Johnson (tpts.); Bernard Raphael, Honore Dutrey (tbns.); Paul Beaullieaux, Sam Dutrey, Sr. (clts.); Alphonse Vache (b.h.); Willie Phillips (s.d.).

Olympia Brass Band (ca. 1960–)—10 pieces: Ernest Cagnolatti, George "Kid Shiek" Colar, Andrew Anderson, Milton Batiste (tpts.); Albert Warner, Louis Nelson, Roger James, Paul Crawford, Homer Eugene (tbns.); Harold Dejan (leader, alto sax); Jesse Charles, Emanuel Paul (tenor saxes); Louis Cottrell, Jr. (clt.); Jim Young, Anderson Minor, William Grant Brown (b.h.); Josiah "CiE" Frazier, Andrew Jefferson (s.d.); Henry "Booker T" Glass, Nowell "Papa" Glass (b.d.).

Onward Brass Band (ca. 1885–1930)—10–12 pieces: Manuel Perez (leader); Andrew Kimble, Peter Bocage, Oscar

Ducongé, James McNeil, Bellevue Lenair, Sylvester Coustaut, Joe Oliver, Maurice Durand (tpts.); Buddy Johnson, Vic Gaspard, George Fihle, Baptiste Deslisle, Steve Johnson, Earl Humphrey, Butler Rapp (tbns.); Lorenzo Tio, Jr., Luis Tio, George Baquet (clts.); Joseph Bruno, Isidore Barbarin, Adolphe Alexander, Sr., Bartholomew Brun (alto horns); Eddie Atkins, Aaron Clark, Joseph Clark, Sr. (baritone horns); Eddie Jackson, Frank Jackson, Albert Tucker (b.h.); Bebé Matthews, Dee Dee Chandler (s.d.); "Black Benny" Williams, Henry Martin, Dandy Lewis, Mike Gillen, Clay Jiles, Christopher "Black Happy" Goldston (b.d.).

(Revived) Onward Brass Band (1960–): Alvin Alcorn, Albert Waters, Theodore Riley (tpts.); Wendell Eugene, Homer Eugene (tbns.); Louis Cottrell, Jr. (clt.); Oscar Rouzan (alto sax); Jerry Green (b.h.); Placide Adams (s.d.); Chester Jones, Paul Barbarin (b.d.).

Pacific Brass Band (*ca*. 1900–1930)—10 pieces: George Hooker, Joe Lizard, Manuel Manetta, Kid Rena, Elmer Talbert, Eddie Vincent (tpts.); Buddy Johnson, Frank Duson (tbns.); Dude Gabriel, George Lewis (clts.); George Sims (baritone horn); James A. Palao (alto horn); Manny Gabriel (alto sax); Bobo Lewis (b.h.); Duke Simpson (s.d.); George Davis, Edgar Moseley (b.d.).

Pickwick Brass Band (*ca*. 1898–1901): Norman Manetta (leader, tpt.); Jules Manetta (tpt.); Edward Love (tbn.); Levi Bailey (flute); Dennis Williams, Tate Rouchon (b.h.).

Reliance Brass Band (*ca*. 1892–1918): Manuel Mello, Fred Neuroth, Joe Lala, Johnny Lala, Richard Brunies, Gus Zimmerman, Merritt Brunies, Albert Brunies, Nick LaRocca, Pete Pellegrini, Frank Christian, Lawrence Veca, George Barth, Harry Shannon, Pete Dientrans, Ray Lopez, Johnny DeDroit (tpts.); Leonce Mello, Dave Perkins, Eddie Edwards, George Brunies, Emile Christian, Marcus Kahn, Bill Gallaty,

Sr., Ricky Toms, Jules Cassard, Henry Brunies, Tom Brown, "Happy" Schilling (tbns.); "Yellow" Nunez, Achille Baquet, Martin Hirsch, Sidney Moore, Clem Camp, Johnny Fischer, Larry Shields, Tony Giardina, Gus Meuller, John Paliser, Red Rowling, Leon Roppolo, Sr. (clts.); Alfred Laine, Vincent Barocco, Merritt Brunies (alto horns); Manuel Belasco (baritone horn); Joe Alexander, "Chink Martin" (b.h.); Jack Laine (leader); Tim Harris, "Ragbaby" Stevens, Johnny Stein, Tony Sbarbaro, Billy Lambert, Diddie Stephens, Emmett Rogers (d.).

St. Joseph Brass Band (*ca*. 1888–1895)—Donaldsonville, La.: Claiborne Williams (leader); William Dalley, Sullivan Sproul, Edward Duffy, Israel Palmer, Lawrence Hall (tpts.); George Williams, Ernest Hime, Harrison Homer (tbns.); Marble Gibson, Ben Baddeurs (clts.); Jim Williams (b.s.); Joe Walker, Buddy Curry, "Bow Legs" (d.).

Terminal Brass Band (*ca*. 1900–1910): Harrison Barnes, Paul Pierre, Louis Rodriguez, George Brashear (tpts.); Joseph Petit, Sunny Henry, Joe Smith (tbns.); Willie Parker (clt.); Clem Brown, "Pompey" (alto horns); "Shiek-O" (baritone horn); Joe Parker (b.h.); Joe Marin (s.d.); Man Creole, Henry Robertson (b.d.).

Tuxedo Brass Band (1910–1925)—10 pieces: Oscar Celestin (leader); Manuel Perez, Mutt Carey, Louis Dumaine, Alcide Landry, Charlie Love, Joe Howard, Willie Pajaud, Louis Armstrong, Peter Bocage, Dee Dee Pierce, Amos White, Maurice Durand, "Kid Shots" Madison (tpts.); Baba Ridgley, Buddy Johnson, Yank Johnson, Sunny Henry, Hamp Benson, Harrison Barnes, Eddie Atkins, Jim Robinson, Loochie Jackson (tbns.); Alphonse Picou, Sam Dutrey, Sr., Lorenzo Tio, Jr., Lorenzo Tio, Sr., Johnny Dodds, Jimmie Noone (clts.); Isidore Barbarin, Louis Keppard (alto horns); George Hooker, Adolphe Alexander, Sr. (baritone horns); Joe Howard (b.h.); Abby "Chinee" Foster, Zutty Singleton,

Christopher "Black Happy" Goldston, Louis Cottrell, Sr. (s.d.); Ernest Trapagnier, "Black Benny" Williams (b.d.).

Abby Williams Happy Pals (*ca*. 1948–1952): Dee Dee Pierce, Kid Howard, Kid Clayton (tpts.); Eddie Pierson, Jim Robinson (tbns.); "Tats" Alexander (clt.); Jesse Charles (sax); Noon Johnson (b.h.); Abby Williams (leader, s.d.); Chester Jones (b.d.).

George Williams Brass Band (*ca*. 1948–): Albert Waters, Alvin Alcorn, Theodore Riley, Ernest Cagnolatti (tpts.); Buster Moore, Worthia Thomas (tbns.); Steve Angram (clt.); Ernest Poree (alto sax); Jesse Charles (tenor sax); William Brown (b.h.); Edmund Washington (s.d.); Josiah "CiE" Frazier, George Williams (leader, b.d.).

Youka Brass Band (*ca*. 1905)—Thibodeaux, La.: Lewis Farrel, Joe Bank, Willie Young (tpts.); Bud Green (clt.); Alfred Dixon (alto horn); Henry Jules, Adam Wallace (baritone horns); Lawrence Jules (tbn.); Albert Jiles, Sr. (s.d.); Clay Jiles (b.d.).

Young Tuxedo Brass Band (*ca*. 1935–)—10 pieces: Alvin Alcorn, Kid Howard, Thomas Jefferson, "Kid Shots" Madison, Edgar Joseph, Dee Dee Pierce, Vernon Gilbert, John Brunious, Andrew Anderson (tpts.); Sunny Henry, Joe Avery, Loochie Jackson, Albert Warner, Clement Tervalon, Wendell Eugene (tbns.); John Casimir (leader, clt.); Albert Burbank (clt.); Adolphe Alexander, Jr., Andrew Morgan, John Handy (saxes); Eddie Jackson, Wilbert Tillman (b.h.); Ernest Rogers, Edmund Washington, Emile Knox, Josiah "CiE" Frazier, Paul Barbarin, Alfred Williams (d.).

Bibliography

The following materials deal with the band movement in America, New Orleans brass bands, and the history of early jazz. They have been useful in compiling this book and may be of value for further study on the subject.

Berger, Kenneth, ed. *Band Encyclopedia*. Evansville, Ind.: Band Associates, Inc., 1960.

Blesh, Rudi. *Shining Trumpets: A History of Jazz*. New York: Alfred A. Knopf, 1946.

Bridges, Glenn. *Pioneers in Brass*. Detroit: Sherwood Publications, 1968.

Brunn, H. O. *The Story of the Original Dixieland Jazz Band*. Baton Rouge: Louisiana State University Press, 1960.

Camus, Raoul F. "A Re-evaluation of the American Band Tradition," *Journal of Band Research*, VII (Fall, 1970), 5–6.

Carroll, George P. "The Band of Musick of the Second Virginia Regiment," *Journal of Band Research*, II (Spring, 1966), 16–18.

Carse, Adam. *Musical Wind Instruments*. New York: Da Capo Press, 1965.

Charters, Samuel B. *Jazz: New Orleans, 1885–1957*. Belleville, N. J.: Walter C. Allen, 1958.

———. Notes to *The Music of New Orleans, Vol 2, Music of the Eureka Brass Band*. Folkways Records FA 2642.

Chilton, John. *Who's Who of Jazz*. Philadelphia: Chilton Book Co., 1972.

Crouch, Rebekah E. "The Contributions of Adolphe Sax to the Wind Band," *Journal of Band Research*, Pt. I, V (Spring, 1969), 29–42; Pt. II, VI (Fall, 1969), 59–65.

Eliason, Robert E. *Graves and Company, Musical Instrument Makers*. Dearborn, Mich.: Henry Ford Museum, n.d.

———. *Keyed Bugles in the United States*. Washington: Smithsonian Institution Press, 1972.

Felts, Jack. "Some Aspects of the Rise and Development of the Wind Band During the Civil War," *Journal of Band Research*, III (Spring, 1966), 29–33.

Fennell, Frederick. "The Civil War: Its Music and Its Sounds," *Journal of Band Research*, Pt. I, IV (Spring, 1968), 36–48; Pt. II, V (Fall, 1968), 8–14, and V (Spring, 1969), 4–10.

———. Notes to *The Civil War*, Vol. 1, Mercury Records LSP2-501, and Vol. 2, LSP2-502.

Gara, Larry, *The Baby Dodds Story*. Los Angeles: Contemporary Press, 1959.

Goffin, Robert. *Jazz: From the Congo to the Metropolitan*. New York: Doubleday Doran, 1944.

———. *La Nouvelle-Orléans Capitale du Jazz*. New York: Éditions de la Maison Française, 1946.

Hall, Harry H. "The Moravian Wind Ensemble Tradition in America," *Journal of Band Research*, I (Winter, 1965), 27–29.

Harris, Rex. *Jazz*. 4th rev. ed. London: Harmondsworth, 1956.

Intravaia, Lawrence J. "The Historical Development of the March as an Art Form," *Journal of Band Research*, IV (Autumn, 1967), 4–11.

Kmen, Henry A. *Music in New Orleans: The Formative Years, 1791–1841*. Baton Rouge: Louisiana State University Press, 1966.

———. "The Music of New Orleans," in Hodding Carter, ed. *The Past as Prelude: New Orleans, 1718–1968*. New Orleans: Tulane University, 1968.

LaCour, Arthur Burton. *New Orleans Masquerade*. New Orleans: Pelican Publishing Co., 1957.

Lomax, Alan. *Mister Jelly Roll*. New York: Duell, Sloan and Pearce, 1950.

Mayer, Francis N. "Nineteenth Century American Band Music," *Music Educators Journal*, Pt. I, XLV (January, 1959), 42, 44, 46; Pt. II, XLV (February-March, 1959), 40, 42.

Mellers, Wilfrid. *Music in a New Found Land*. New York: Alfred A. Knopf, 1967.

Meryman, Richard. *Louis Armstrong—A Self-Portrait*. New York: Eakins Press, 1971.

Ramsey, Frederic, Jr. Notes to *Music from the South, Vol. 1: Country Brass Bands*. Folkways Records FP650.

Ramsey, Frederic, Jr., and Charles Edward Smith. *Jazzmen*. New York: Harcourt, Brace and Co., 1939.

Rose, Al, and Edmond Souchon. *New Orleans Jazz: A Family Album*. Baton Rouge: Louisiana State University Press, 1967.

Saxon, Lyle, *et al. Gumbo Ya Ya*. Boston: Houghton Mifflin, 1945.

Schuller, Gunther. *Early Jazz: Its Roots and Musical Development*. New York: Oxford University Press, 1968.

Schwartz, H. W. *Bands of America*. Garden City, N.J.: Doubleday and Co., 1957.

Shapiro, Nat, and Nat Hentoff. *Hear Me Talkin' to Ya*. New York: Rinehart, 1955.

Smith, Charles Edward. "New Orleans and Traditions in Jazz," in Nat Hentoff and Albert McCarthy, eds. *Jazz*. New York: Grove Press, 1961.

Specht, Paul M. *How They Became Name Bands*. New York: Fine Arts Publications, 1941.

Stackhouse, David L. "D. W. Reeves and His Music," *Journal of Band Research*, Pt. I, V (Spring, 1969), 15–28.

Stagg, Tom, and Charlie Crump. *New Orleans: The Revival*. Dublin: Bashall Eaves, 1973.

Stoddard, Tom. *The Autobiography of Pops Foster*. Los Angeles: University of California Press, 1971.

Trotter, James M. *Music and Some Highly Musical People*. Boston: Lee and Shepard, 1878.

White, William C. *History of Military Music in America*. New York: Exposition Press, 1944.

Williams, Martin, ed. *Jazz Panorama*. New York: Collier Books, 1964.

Zander, Majorie Thomas. "The Brass-Band Funeral and Related Negro Burial Customs." M.A. thesis, University of North Carolina, Chapel Hill, 1962.

Discography

What follows is a listing of microgroove recordings, many no longer readily available, of all known commercial issues. For details on unissued recordings, films, and television productions, see Tom Stagg and Charlie Crump, *New Orleans, The Revival* (Dublin: Bashall Eaves, 1973).

Bunk's Brass Band: William G. "Bunk" Johnson, "Kid Shots" Madison (tpts.), Jim Robinson (tbn.), Isidore Barbarin (alto horn), Adolphe Alexander, Sr. (baritone horn), George Lewis (clt.), Joseph "Red" Clark (b.h.), Warren "Baby" Dodds (s.d.), Lawrence Marrero (b.d.). Recorded May 18, 1945.

> American Music LP 643, Dixie LP 107, Storyville SLP 202, Dan (Japanese) VC 7011: "When the Saints Go Marching In," "Just a Little While to Stay Here," "Nearer My God to Thee."
>
> American Music LP 638, Storyville SLP 202, Dan (Japanese) VC 7011: "Just a Closer Walk with Thee."
>
> Dixie LP 107, Folkways FP 57, F.J. 2803, Storyville SLP 202, Dan (Japanese) VC 7011: "Over in the Gloryland," "You Tell Me Your Dream."
>
> American Music Baby Dodds No. 4: "Bye and Bye."

E. Gibson Brass Band: Eddie Richardson, Johnny Wimberley, Sr., John Henry McNeil (tpts.), Carroll "Cal" Blunt, Eddie Noble (tbns.), Robert Davis (alto sax), Alphonse Spears (tenor sax and manager), Albert Miller (b.h.), George Sterling (s.d.), Dave Bailey (b.d.). Recorded November 16, 1963.

> M.O.N.O. (British) MNLP 6: "Come Ye Disconsolate," "What a Friend We Have in Jesus," "Lord, Lord, Lord," "The Shiek of Araby," "Bye and Bye," "Shanty in Old Shanty Town," "Just a Little While to Stay Here," "The Little Rascal," "Jesus on the Main Line," "When the Saints Go Marching In," "You Tell Me Your Dream."

Eureka Brass Band: Percy Humphrey, Willie Pajaud, Eddie Richardson (tpts.), Sunny Henry, Albert Warner (tbns.), Ruben Roddy (alto sax), Emanuel Paul (tenor sax), George Lewis (E♭ clt.), Joseph "Red" Clark (b.h.), Arthur Ogle (s.d.), Robert Lewis (b.d.). Recorded August, 1951.

> Pax 9001, Melodisc (British) MLP 12-101: "Garlands of Flowers," "Sing On," "West Lawn Dirge," "Lady Be Good."
>
> Folkways FA 2465: "You Tell Me Your Dream."
>
> *The Eureka Brass Band in Rehearsal*, New Orleans Rarities 4: "Panama," "Unknown Hymn," "Just a Little While to Stay Here," "Sweet Fields," "Down in Honky Tonk Town," "Lord, Lord, Lord."
>
> *Music of the Eureka Brass Band*, Folkways FA 2462: "Panama."

Percy Humphrey, Willie Pajaud, George "Kid Shiek" Colar (tpts.), Sunny Henry, Albert Warner (tbns.), Ruben Roddy (alto sax), Emanuel Paul (tenor sax), Joseph "Red" Clark (b.h.), Alfred Williams (s.d.), Robert Lewis (b.d.).

> *Music of the Eureka Brass Band*: Folkways FA 2462: "Trombonium," "Just a Little While to Stay Here,"

"Lord, Lord, Lord," "Eternity," "Maryland, My Maryland."

Percy Humphrey, Willie Pajaud, George "Kid Shiek" Colar (tpts.), Sunny Henry, Albert Warner (tbns.), Ruben Roddy (alto sax), Emanuel Paul (tenor sax), John Casimir, Alphonse Picou (clts.), Joseph "Red" Clark (b.h.), Alfred Williams (s.d.), Robert Lewis (b.d.).

Music of the South, Vol. 10—Been Here and Gone, Folkways FA 2659: "When the Saints Go Marching In," "Bourbon Street Parade," "Just a Closer Walk with Thee," "Panama."

Percy Humphrey, George "Kid Shiek" Colar, Peter Bocage (tpts.), Albert Warner, Oscar "Chicken" Henry (tbns.), Emanuel Paul (tenor sax), Willie Humphrey (clt.), Wilbert Tillman (b.h.), Josiah "CiE" Frazier (s.d.), Robert Lewis (b.d.). Recorded June 2, 1962.

Atlantic 1408, London (British) EHA-K 8162: "Just a Little While to Stay Here," "Bye and Bye," "Whoopin' Blues," "Down in Honky Tonk Town," "Take Your Burden to the Lord," "Joe Avery's Blues," "Panama."

Alvin Alcorn, Albert "Fernandez" Walters, George "Kid Shiek" Colar (tpts.), Oscar "Chicken" Henry, Earl Humphrey (tbns.), Emanuel Paul (tenor sax), Paul "Polo" Barnes (E♭ clt.), William Grant Brown (b.h.), Nowell "Papa" Glass (s.d.), Henry "Booker T" Glass (b.d.). Recorded January 24, 1968.

Sounds of New Orleans SNO 1: "West Lawn Dirge," "Fallen Heroes," "Nearer My God to Thee."

Jazzlife I, Metronome JEB 1000: "Just a Closer Walk with Thee." No details.

George Lewis Funeral: This recording (French Barclay 920.161) was made of music played on January 3, 1969, for George Lewis' funeral procession and includes the Eureka Brass Band ("What a Friend We Have in Jesus"), an unnamed brass band ("Nearer My God to Thee"), the Olympia Brass Band ("Just a Closer Walk with Thee," "Westlawn Dirge," "What a Friend We Have in Jesus" and "When the Saints Go Marching In").

Kid Rena's Jazz Band: (Although this is not a brass band recording, it includes many of the earlier generation of brass-band musicians playing a repertoire and in the style of the street bands. As the earliest of the New Orleans revival documentary recordings, it is of considerable historical interest.)

Henry "Kid" Rena (tpt.), Jim Robinson (tbn.), Alphonse Picou, Louis Nelson Deslisle (clts.), Willie Santiago (guitar), Albert Glenny (bass), Joe Rena (d.). Recorded August 21, 1940.

Circle L 409, Esquire (British) 10-111, Riverside RLP 1060 and 12-119, Joker SM 3095, BYG (French) 529.062: "Panama," "Gettysburg March," "Milneburg Joys," "Lowdown Blues," "High Society Rag," "Clarinet Marmalade," "Weary Blues," "Get It Right."

(Harold Dejan's) Olympia Brass Band. Ernest Cagnolatti, George "Kid Shiek" Colar (tpts.), Albert Warner, Louis Nelson (tbns.), Harold Dejan (alto sax and leader), Jesse Charles (tenor sax), Louis Cottrell, Jr. (clt.), Anderson Minor (b.h.), Josiah "CiE" Frazier (s.d.), Henry "Booker T" Glass (b.d.). Recorded February 5, 1962.

M.O.N.O. (British) LP 5: "Panama," "Over in the Gloryland," "Lord, Lord, Lord," "What a Friend We Have in Jesus." Includes interviews with Harold Dejan and George "Kid Shiek" Colar.

M.O.N.O. (British) MNLP 16: "Lord, Lord, Lord" (alternative take)

Jazz Crusade JC 2001: "Over in the Gloryland" (alternative take)

Andrew Anderson, Milton Batiste (tpts.), Paul Crawford, Roger James (tnbs.), Harold Dejan (alto sax and leader), Emanuel Paul (tenor sax), Jim Young (b.h.), Anderson Jefferson (s.d.), Henry "Booker T" Glass (b.d.). Recorded June 25, 1968.

> 77 (British) LEU 12/31: "Lord, Lord, Lord," "Olympia Special," "Telephone to Glory," "Second Line," "St. Louis Blues," "West Lawn Dirge," "Bugle Boy March," "She'll Be Comin' Round the Mountain," "E-flat Blues."
>
> M.O.N.O. (British) MNLP 16: "On the Square."

Andrew Anderson, Milton Batiste, Clive Wilson (tpts.), Paul Crawford, Frank Naundorf (tbns.), Harold Dejan (alto sax and leader), Emanuel Paul (tenor sax), Dick Cook (clt.), Klaus Enfield, (b.h.), Andrew Jefferson, Trevor Richards (s.d.), Henry "Booker T" Glass (b.d.). Recorded June 26, 1968.

> NoLa LP 4: "Just a Little While to Stay Here," "Lily of the Valley," "Shiek of Araby," "Over in the Gloryland," "Lead Me Savior," "Just a Closer Walk with Thee," "Lord, Lord, Lord," "The Royal Telephone," "What a Friend We Have in Jesus," "Second Line," "Bourbon Street Parade."
>
> NoLa JBS 2: "Take Your Burden to the Lord," "Tiger Rag."

Andrew Anderson, Milton Batiste, Clive Wilson (tpts.), Paul Crawford, Frank Naundorf (tbns.), Harold Dejan (alto sax and leader), Emanuel Paul (tenor sax), Dick Cook (clt.), Klaus Enfield (b.h.), Andrew Jefferson, Trevor Richards (s.d.), Henry "Booker T" Glass (b.d.). Recorded August 1, 1968.

> *New Orleans Parade*, Saba (German) MPS 15196 ST

and BASF (American) MC 20678: "Take Your Burden to the Lord," "Over in the Gloryland," "We Shall Walk Through the Streets of the City," "In the Upper Garden," "Shake It and Break It," "Lead Me Savior," "Lily of the Valley," "Olympia Special."

NoLa JBS 1: "Over in the Gloryland," "In the Upper Garden," "Olympia Special."

Milton Batiste, George "Kid Shiek" Colar, Andrew Anderson (tpts.), Homer Eugene, Paul Crawford (tbns.), Harold Dejan (alto sax and leader), Emanuel Paul (tenor sax), William Grant Brown (b.h), Andrew Jefferson (s.d.), Henry "Booker T" Glass (b.d.).Recorded Spring, 1971.

> *The Olympia Brass Band of New Orleans*, Audiophile AP 108: Explanation of funeral procession, "Just a Little While to Stay Here," "Dirge" ("Flee as a Bird," "Nearer My God to Thee," "Pleyel's Hymn"), "Just a Closer Walk with Thee," "Telephone to Glory," "Oh, Didn't He Ramble," "Weary Blues," "Panama," "Yes, Sir, That's My Baby," "Willie the Weeper."

Milton Batiste (tpt.), Paul Crawford, Mike Casimir (tbns.), Harold Dejan (alto sax and leader), Joseph Torregano (clt.), Irvin Eisen (b.h.), Andrew Jefferson (s.d.), Nowell "Papa" Glass (b.d.). Recorded November 21, 1972.

> NoLa JBS (S) 3: "New Second Line," "Basin Street Blues/The Duck's Yas Yas."

Onward Brass Band: Ernest Cagnolatti, Albert "Fernandez" Walters, Avery "Kid" Howard (tpts.), Clement Tervalon, Worthia Thomas (tbns.), Harold Dejan (alto sax), Andrew Morgan (tenor sax), Joshua Willis (mellophone), Joseph "Cornbread" Thomas (clt.), Anderson Minor (b.h.), Louis Barbarin, Placide Adams (s.d.), Paul Barbarin (b.d.). Recorded January 23, 1965.

> *Last Journey of a Jazzman (The Funeral of Lester Santi-*

ago), Vol. I/II, Nobility LP 708, 709: "Just a Little While to Stay Here," "What a Friend We Have in Jesus," "Lead Me Savior," "Just a Closer Walk with Thee," "Nearer My God to Thee," "Lead Me Savior (Medley)," "Just a Closer Walk with Thee (Medley)," "Abide with Me," "When the Saints Go Marching In," "Bourbon Street Parade," "Bill Bailey," "Second Line," "Darktown Strutters' Ball."

Alvin Alcorn, Ernest Cagnolatti (tpts.), Clement Tervalon, Wendell Eugene (tbns.), Louis Cottrell, Jr. (clt.), Jerry Green (b.h.), Freddie Kohlman (s.d.), Paul Barbarin (b.d., leader), Danny Barker (banjo, grand marshall). Recorded June 27, 1968.

> Connecticut Jazz Club SLP 5: "Maryland, My Maryland," "Just a Closer Walk with Thee," "Second Line," "Original Dixieland One-Step."

Original Zenith Brass Band: Avery "Kid" Howard, Peter Bocage (tpts.), Jim Robinson (tbn.), Isidore Barbarin (mellophone), Harrison Barnes (baritone horn), George Lewis (E♭ clt.), Joe Howard (b.h.), Warren "Baby" Dodds (s.d.), Lawrence Marrero (b.d.). Recorded February 26, 1946.

> Esquire (British) 10-172, Riverside RLP 12-283: "Fidgety Feet," "Shake It and Break It," "Bugle Boy March," "Salutation March," "If I Ever Cease to Love," "'Tain't Nobody's Biz-ness If I Do."

Young Tuxedo Brass Band: Albert "Fernandez" Walters, John "Pickey" Brunious, Andrew Anderson (tpts.), Clement Tervalon, Jim Robinson, Eddie Pierson (tbns.), Herman Sherman (alto sax), Andrew Morgan (tenor sax), John Casimir (E♭ clt.), Wilbert Tillman (b.h.), Paul Barbarin (s.d.), Emile Knox (b.d.). Recorded August 31 and November 2, 1958.

> *Jazz Begins*, Atlantic 1297, London (British) LTZ-K 15234, SAH-K 6202, Atlantic (French) 372006: "Lead Me Savior," "Eternal Peace," "Medley of Hymns ("Flee as a Bird," "Nearer My God to Thee," "Pleyel's Hymn"), "Just a Closer Walk with Thee," "Bourbon Street Parade," "Lord, Lord, Lord," "Just a Little While to Stay Here," "Panama," "It Feels So Good," "Joe Avery's Piece," "John Casimir's Whoopin' Blues."

Andrew Anderson (tpt.), Bill Matthews, Oscar "Chicken" Henry (tbns.), John Handy (alto sax), Jesse Charles (tenor sax), John Casimir (E♭ clt.), Wilbert Tillman (b.h.), Alfred Williams (s.d.), William Philip (b.d.). Recorded September, 1960.

> M.O.N.O. (British) MNLP 16: "When the Saints Go Marching In."

A recording of related historical interest is *Music from the South, Vol. 1: Country Brass Bands*, Folkways FP 650, which documents two rural brass bands in Alabama in 1954.

> Laneville-Johnson Union Brass Band: "Precious Lord, Hold My Hand," "Take Rocks and Gravel to Build a Solid Road," "Wild About My Daddy," "Sun Gonna Shine in My Back Door Some Day," "I'm Goin' On," "O Lord Let Your Will Be Done," "Preaching Tonight on the Old Camp Ground," "My Baby Gone and She Won't Be Back No More," "Fare You Well, Daddy, It's Your Time Now."

> Lapsey Band: "Sing On," "Dixie," "Going Up the Country, Don't You Want to Go," "I Shall Not Be Moved," "The Ship Is Over the Ocean," "Mama, Don't You Tear My Clothes," "Nearer My God to Thee," "Like My Lord," "I'm All Right Now Since I've Been Converted," "Just Over in the Gloryland," "When I Lay My Burden Down."

Appendix II **Musical Materials**

"Fallen Heroes"

The score reproduced is a facsimile of the 1894 printing of George Southwell's dirge, a long-time favorite of New Orleans street bands, including the Onward Brass Band (with Manuel Perez playing the solo B^b cornet part) and the Eureka Brass Band, where it was known as "Number 31." "Fallen Heroes" is typical of the nineteenth-century dirges composed and published across the country, in constant demand by military and quasimilitary bands.

These pieces were composed for average amateur brass bands; therefore, they could not be overly complex or laden with difficult technical demands. On the other hand, the dirges had to be properly melancholy, deliberate, and melodic. "Fallen Heroes" shows how a journeyman composer in this idiom met these specifications.

Dirges followed simple conventions. "Fallen Heroes" is highly tuneful, with a Gallic operatic lilt. It is simple in form, consisting of three brief, closely related melodic strains or movements. The first section of thirty-two bars introduces the main melodic unit, which is repeated and developed in various forms throughout. The motif, from the solo B^b cornet part, is:

(measures 1–3)

The basic rhythmic pattern here—  —defines the melody and the dirge motion of the music. This dotted rhythm is opposed to another rhythmic pattern in the drums and alto-tenor horn choirs—

The tension between dotted and off-beat rhythmic patterns provides the slow but lyrical motion. The basic motif alters slightly at the beginning of the third eight-bar segment (measures 17–18)—

This change leads to a further evolution of the motif in the second strain (measures 33–34)—

so that the dirge gradually develops from its plain opening motif through the complex melody of its concluding trio.

The trio strain is the capstone of the dirge; the second strain of eight bars, repeated, reiterates the modified opening theme and leads directly to the song-like feeling of the trio, with its deep-throated baritone horn solo. The trio begins with an introductory flourish—

—recalling the first dotted figure and its suggestion of a bugle-call. The music, through these figures, assumes a martial character that combines with the lyrical feeling to create an interesting melodic quality, like that of standard French dirges of the early nineteenth century.

The solo baritone horn part of the trio strain climaxes "Fallen Heroes." It brings a resonant middle-range voice into the melodic line, earlier carried most assertively by cornets and clarinets. The dirge closes rapidly after this brief baritone horn solo—in practice it was probably repeated *da capo* several times when played on the march, returning to the repetitive first motif. The over-all feeling is martial and distinctly brassy, with emphasis on the middle-register cornet line and the lower baritone voice. It is not a virtuoso piece of *bel canto* work but a smoothly fluid *cantabile* line, restrained but not severe.

The parts reveal how stolid and simple writing for dirges can be. Most instruments play in unison harmony the main melodic line; the alto and tenor horns, coupled with bass and drums, accompany the melodic line with very simple rhythmic off-beat figures. The rest of the band plays the melody line in various stages of complexity. The effect is of a massive organ-like sound—solid and full, but without complex contrapuntal or harmonic effects and designed for a chorale-like effect. The emphasis on the lower range of the band—apparent at the eighth bar with the bass solo line— keeps the somber, unspectacular mood intact, without the wailing or keening sound of some dirges.

As played by New Orleans street bands after 1900, the parts for obsolete tenor horns, E^b cornet, second alto and baritone horns, piccolo, and multiple clarinets would have been omitted. The three B^b cornet parts would have been emphasized, along with the E^b clarinet. These instruments would have carried the main burden, and the lyrical B^b solo cornet part would have been the outstanding component in performance. Cornet and baritone horn would have shared the honor of the climactic solo in the trio, and "Fallen Heroes" would emerge as less massively solid and more lyrical in performance by a ten-piece band in the hands of a skilled reading musician like Manuel Perez, Southwell's dirge would have worked as an effective and evocative piece of funeral music, even with a small ensemble. The printed sheets do not reveal the nuances of performance that a spirited soloist could render, but they do exemplify the musical materials from which New Orleans brass bands worked.

FUNERAL MARCH.
(FALLEN HEROES.)

Eb Cornet.

GEO. SOUTHWELL.

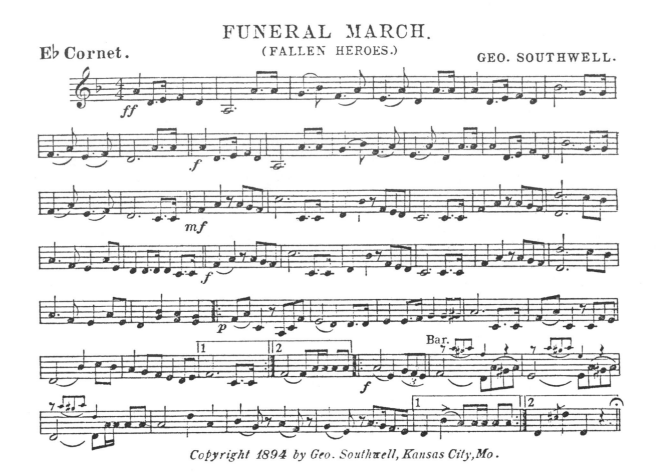

Copyright 1894 by Geo. Southwell, Kansas City, Mo.

FUNERAL MARCH.
(FALLEN HEROES.)

Solo B♭ Cornet.

GEO. SOUTHWELL.

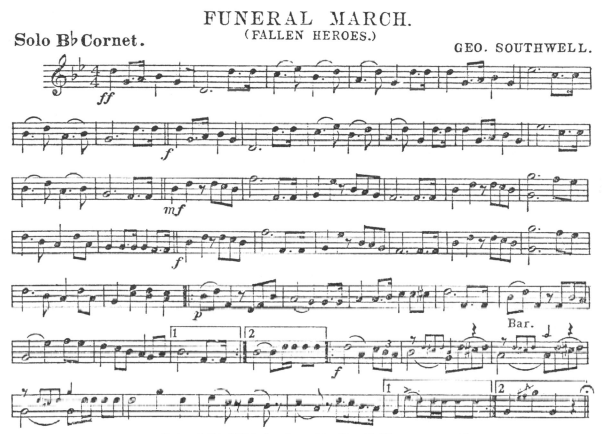

FUNERAL MARCH.
(FALLEN HEROES.)

1st B♭ Cornet.

GEO. SOUTHWELL.

Geo. Southwell, Publisher, Kansas City, Mo.

FUNERAL MARCH.
(FALLEN HEROES.)

2d B♭ Cornet.

GEO. SOUTHWELL.

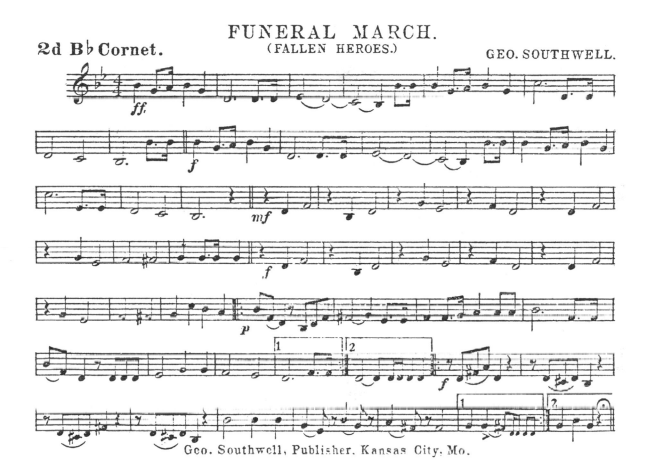

Geo. Southwell, Publisher, Kansas City, Mo.

FUNERAL MARCH.
(FALLEN HEROES.)

E♭ Clarinet.

GEO. SOUTHWELL.

Geo. Southwell, Publisher, Kansas City, Mo.

FUNERAL MARCH.
(FALLEN HEROES.)

Piccolo.

GEO. SOUTHWELL.

Geo. Southwell, Publisher, Kansas City, Mo.

FUNERAL MARCH.
(FALLEN HEROES.)

1st B♭ Clarinet.

GEO. SOUTHWELL.

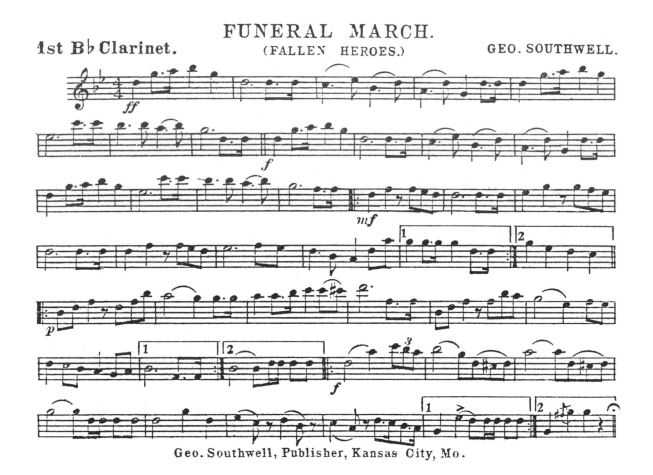

Geo. Southwell, Publisher, Kansas City, Mo.

FUNERAL MARCH.
(FALLEN HEROES.)

2d Bb Clarinet.

GEO. SOUTHWELL.

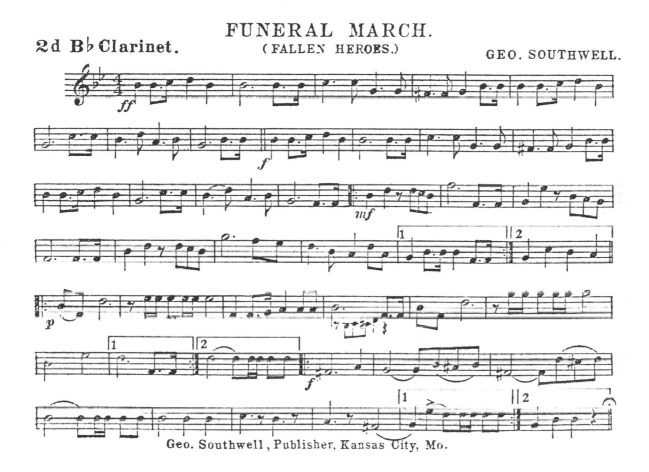

Geo. Southwell, Publisher, Kansas City, Mo.

FUNERAL MARCH.
FALLEN HEROES.)

1st & 2d B♭ Tenors.

GEO. SOUTHWELL.

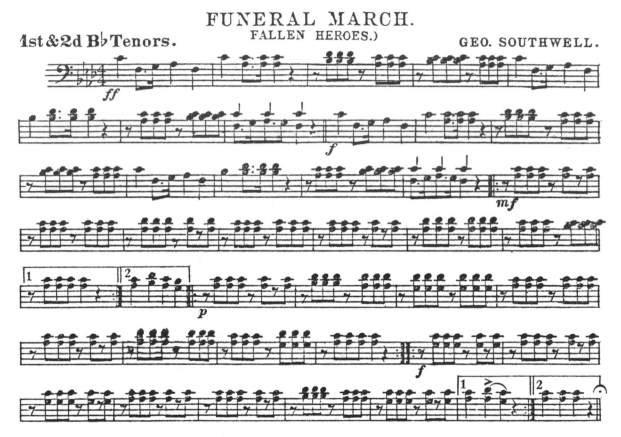

Geo. Southwell, Publisher, Kansas City, Mo.

FUNERAL MARCH.
FALLEN HEROES.)

Baritone.

GEO. SOUTHWELL.

Geo. Southwell, Publisher, Kansas City, Mo.

FUNERAL MARCH.
(FALLEN HEROES.)

Solo Bb Trombone.

GEO. SOUTHWELL.

Geo. Southwell, Publisher, Kansas City. Mo.

FUNERAL MARCH.
(FALLEN HEROES.)

Solo Alto.

GEO. SOUTHWELL.

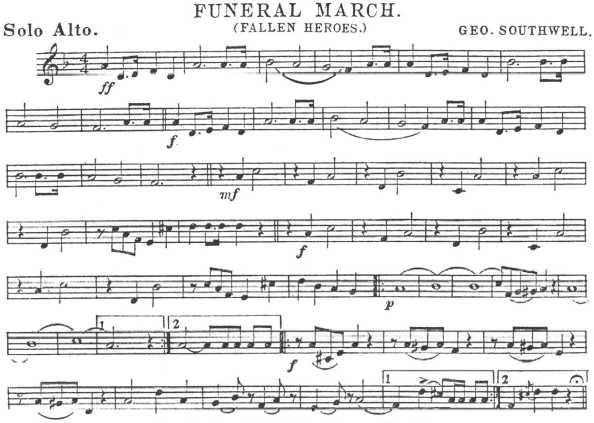

Geo. Southwell, Publisher, Kansas City, Mo.

FUNERAL MARCH.
(FALLEN HEROES.)

Baritone.

GEO. SOUTHWELL.

Geo. Southwell, Publisher, Kansas City, Mo.

FUNERAL MARCH.
(FALLEN HEROES.)

1st E♭ Alto.

GEO. SOUTHWELL.

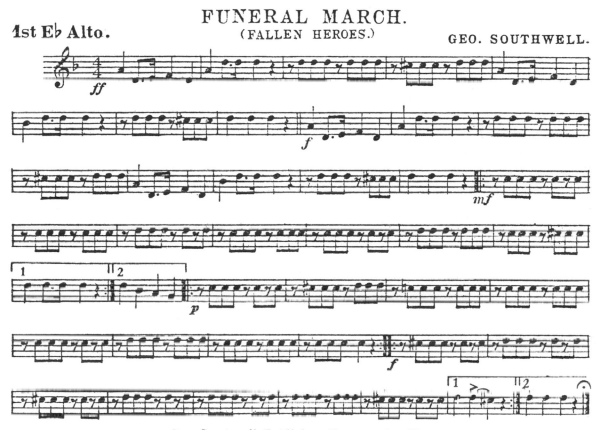

Geo. Southwell, Publisher, Kansas City, Mo.

FUNERAL MARCH.
(FALLEN HEROES.)

2d E♭ Alto.

GEO. SOUTHWELL.

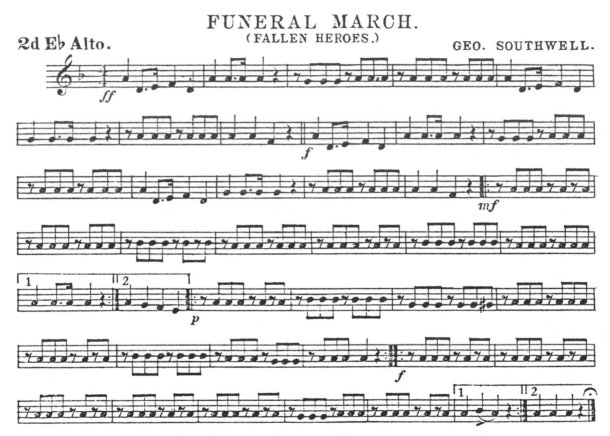

Geo. Southwell, Publisher, Kansas City, Mo.

FUNERAL MARCH.
(FALLEN HEROES.)

Tuba & B♭ Bass.

GEO. SOUTHWELL.

Geo. Southwell, Publisher, Kansas City, Mo.

FUNERAL MARCH.
(FALLEN HEROES.)

GEO. SOUTHWELL.

Drums.
(Muffled.)

Geo. Southwell, Publisher, Kansas City, Mo.

Notes

Chapter One

1 On March 4, 1864, Gilmore presented his "Grand National Concert" in New Orleans, using a brass band of approximately five hundred pieces. H. W. Schwartz, *Bands of America* (Garden City, N.Y.: Doubleday and Co., 1957), 51. One historian of early military music in America asserts that the American band was vital early in the Revolutionary period: "The 3rd and 4th Regiments of Artillery, commanded by Colonels John Crane and Thomas Proctor, had bands as early as 1777, and these served until the end of the war. Both bands achieved reputations of excellence, surpassing any other musical group, civilian or military, in existence at the time, and may alone serve as sufficient basis of an American military musical tradition." Raoul F. Camus, "A Reevaluation of the American Band Tradition," *Journal of Band Research*, VII (Fall, 1970), 6. See also George P. Carroll, "The Band of Musick of the Second Virginia Regiment," *Journal of Band Research*, II (Spring, 1966), 16–18.
2 Lawrence J. Intravaia, "The Historical Development of the March as an Art Form," *Journal of Band Research*, IV (Autumn, 1967), 7.
3 The miscellaneous nature of band organization is illustrated by the United States Marine Band, which claims to be the oldest continuously operated band in America. Its origin was very simple: "The instrumentation of the Marine Band in 1800 consisted of two oboes, two horns, a bassoon, and a drum." Francis N. Mayer, "Early Band Music in the United States," *Music Educators Journal*, XLV (January, 1959), 40.
4 A summary of the Moravian influence on the band tradition is Harry H. Hall, "The Moravian Wind Ensemble Tradition in America," *Journal of Band Research*, I (Winter, 1969), 27–29.
5 A recent commentator explained technical features of the new brass instruments:

In the mid-1840's, a new type of ensemble began to replace the keyed brasses. The saxhorns—noted for their uniformity of sound—were a family of valved, conical brasses (soprano through contrabass) named after one of their developers, Adolphe Sax. Although built in a variety of styles, most saxhorns had these common characteristics: (1) a gradually tapering bore (somewhere between the wide conical taper of the bugle and the more cylindrical tubing of the trumpet) that encouraged the production of a mellow sound throughout the range; (2) rotary or cylindrical valves that allowed ease in obtaining chromatic notes; and (3) evenness in tone quality and production (by eliminating the holes in the tubing, saxhorns avoided what Dodworth called the "lumpiness of tone" of the keyed bugle family and were considered easier to play).

Cynthia Adams Hoover, Notes to *19th-Century American Ballroom Music*, Nonesuch Records H-71313. See also Rebekah E. Crouch, "The Contributions of Adolphe Sax to the Wind Band," Pt. I. *Journal of Band Research*, V (Spring, 1969), 29–42, and Pt. II, *Journal of Band Research*, VI (Fall, 1969), 59–65; and Adam Carse, *Musical Wind Instruments* (New York: Da Capo Press, 1965), Chaps. VII and VIII.
6 See Frederick Fennell's Notes to *The Civil War*, Vol. 1, Mercury Records LSP2-501, p. 6.
7 Jonathan Elkus, *Charles Ives and the American Band Tradition* (Exeter, England: University of Exeter, 1974), 17.
8 Fennell, again in Notes to *The Civil War*, Vol. I, Mercury Records LSP2-501, says that one band whose music has been preserved was the Regiment Band of the 26th North Carolina, recruited intact into the Confederate Army, "originally a Moravian brass band from the Moravian settlement at Salem, North Carolina," p. 5.
9 The decline and reemergence of the slide trombone in the Amer-

ican band is a curious episode, caused evidently by the assumption that valved brass instruments were somehow intrinsically superior to those without the new device:

> By 1853, Dodworth considered trumpets, horns, and trombones expendable, in part because music assigned to them could now be played on cornets, keyed bugles, and saxhorns, and in part because he felt they were played too loudly. Taking strong exception to the trombonists of his time, Dodworth wrote that he agreed with a review of a concert in Manhattan which recommended that for future concerts "the trombones should be placed in Brooklyn."

See Hoover, Notes to *19th-Century American Ballroom Music*, Nonesuch Records H-71313.

10 By the turn of the century cheap but serviceable band instruments were available by mail from merchandisers like Sears, Roebuck, who could supply instrumentation for whole town bands. According to their 1908 catalog, "Last year we furnished over 500 bands with complete sets of instruments besides selling an immense number of single instruments of all kinds, and this year our business will undoubtedly be doubled." *Sears, Roebuck and Co., Catalogue No. 117* (Chicago: Follett Publishing Co., 1969), 248. In this catalog, prices for cornets start at $6.65, trombones at $6.85, clarinets at $9.95.

11 Schwartz, *Bands of America*, 82.

12 In a perhaps over-enthusiastic estimate, a late-nineteenth century writer placed the number of American bands very high and then defined the typical provincial band of his day:

> At present there are over ten thousand military bands in the United States. In smaller cities they average twenty-five men each. In small country towns they number from twelve to eighteen members.
>
> The average band, composed of twenty-five men, is usually made up in this wise: one piccolo, one E flat clarinet, four B flat clarinets, two E flat cornets, four B flat cornets, two alto horns, three trombones or tenor horns, two barytones [*sic*], two tubas, one small drum, a bass drum, and cymbals.

Leon Mead, "The Military Bands of the United States," *Harper's Weekly*, September 28, 1889, p. 785.

13 James M. Trotter, *Music and Some Highly Musical People* (Boston: Lee and Shepard, 1878), 351.

14 New Orleans *Picayune*, February 24, 1885, p. 3, c. 1–3.

15 Gunther Schuller, *Early Jazz: Its Roots and Musical Development* (New York: Oxford University Press, 1968), 25–26.

16 For a complete discussion of the New Orleans musical milieu, see Henry A. Kmen, *Music in New Orleans: The Formative Years, 1791–1841* (Baton Rouge: Louisiana State University Press, 1966).

17 James Haskins, *Pinckney Benton Stewart Pinchback* (New York: Macmillan, 1973), 41–42.

18 *Ibid.*, 144, 191.

19 Henry Clay Warmoth, *War, Politics and Reconstruction* (New York: Macmillan, 1930), 260–62.

20 Jane Julian, "Magnolia's Music," *Mississippi Rag*, July, 1974, pp. 7–8.

21 Rudi Blesh, *Shining Trumpets: A History of Jazz* (New York: Alfred A. Knopf, 1946), 155.

22 John Rublowsky, *Black Music in America* (New York: Basic Books, 1971), 123.

23 The passages quoted are from Frederic Ramsey, Jr., Notes to *Music from the South, Vol. I: Country Brass Bands*, Folkways FP650.

24 Robert C. Toll, *Blacking Up* (New York: Oxford University Press, 1974), 276–77.

25 *Ibid.*, 248–49.

26 *Ibid.*, 250.

27 See H. Wiley Hitchcock, *Music in the United States: A Historical Introduction* (Englewood Cliffs, N.J.: Prentice-Hall, 1969), 43–46.

28 New Orleans *Item*, June 15, 1893, p. 5, c. 6, and June 16, 1893, p. 8, c. 4. The composition of the larger West End concert bands of this period must have been similar to that given for Armand Veazey's Military Band in 1904: nine clarinets, two piccolos, tenor horn, alto sax, baritone sax, eight cornets, four alto horns, two baritone horns, seven trombones, four tubas, four percussion, totaling forty-three musicians. This is basically the instrumentation of a modern wind band. See New Orleans *Item*, December 20, 1904, p. 2, c. 4.

29 *Ibid.*, November 1, 1906, p. 2, c. 1–2.

30 One of the most influential bands was the Mexican Band, which appeared at the New Orleans Cotton States Exposition of 1885, and whose memory was enduring among New Orleans brass bandsmen: "The column was not complete without the famous band of the 8th Mexican Cavalry, directed by Prof. Encarnacion Payen. The band was cheered whenever it chose to play." New Orleans *Picayune*, December 16, 1885, p. 5, c. 2.

31 New Orleans *Item*, November 7, 1906, p. 5, c. 2.

32 *Ibid.*, August 6, 1911, p. 8, c. 4. At the same time black brass

bands presented programs at the various parks for the black population, as indicated by this ad, *ibid.*, April 26, 1906, p. 11, c. 1–2:

"Something Doing Every Sunday"
LINCOLN PARK,
"For Colored."
FREE   SUNDAY, APRIL 29.
BALLOON ASCENSION   *4 p.m.*
—AND—
PARACHUTE LEAP

Open Air Concert
—BY—
Excelsior Brass Band

33 Interview with Charles Love, June 19, 1958, p. 1, in William Ransom Hogan Jazz Archive, Howard-Tilton Memorial Library, Tulane University, New Orleans.
34 Interview with Charles "Sunny" Henry, January 8, 1959, p. 10, in William Ransom Hogan Jazz Archive, Howard-Tilton Memorial Library, Tulane University, New Orleans.
35 *Ibid.*, 1.
36 Interview with William "Baba" Ridgley, June 2, 1959, pp. 17–18, in William Ransom Hogan Jazz Archive, Howard-Tilton Memorial Library, Tulane University, New Orleans.
37 Henry interview, January 8, 1959, p. 24, in Hogan Jazz Archive.
38 The form of the modern American band march coalesced in the late nineteenth century into a complex pattern. The march form, since Sousa, has been basically fixed, and one music historian sees it as a growth from the works of Sousa and D. W. Reeves (1838–1900), his immediate predecessor as a genius of the civilian band:

> The music of Reeves, for the first time, injected not only the concept of fully developed counterpoint, but also the idea of a fixed and predetermined form for the military march. The plan consisted of a balanced double period first section and its matching counterpart which he called the trio, the entire piece to be played all the way through with repeats and then "da capo" without the repeats. There was also an introduction to each half, the first especially being terse and provocative of action. . . . Sousa altered this plan to a forward moving, more dynamic form which did not retrace its steps but proceeded to a climax with the final repetition of the trio, its most important section.

See David L. Stackhouse, "D. W. Reeves and His Music," *Journal of Band Research*, V (Spring, 1969), 19.
39 Interview with Peter Bocage, January 24, 1959, p. 6, in William Ransom Hogan Jazz Archive, Howard-Tilton Memorial Library, Tulane University, New Orleans.
40 *Ibid.*, 6–7.
41 *Ibid.*, 46.
42 *Ibid.*
43 New Orleans *Item*, April 30, 1898, p. 7, c. 4.
44 New Orleans *Picayune*, January 12, 1890, p. 6, c. 2.
45 Alan Lomax, *Mister Jelly Roll* (New York: Duell, Sloan and Pierce, 1950), 12.
46 New Orleans *Picayune*, January 13, 1890, p. 3, c. 3.
47 The management of brass bands seems to have followed a long-standing tradition, by which there was a manager, usually someone in the rhythm section, who took care of bookings, finances, advertising, and a *leader*, usually a trumpet or clarinet player, who was musical director on the job.
48 Maud Cuny-Hare, *Negro Musicians and Their Music* (Washington: Associated Publishers, Inc., 1936), 210–11, 212. The same source mentions another Excelsior Brass Band, which later became known as the "Boston Brass Band," *ca.* 1880.
49 New Orleans *Picayune*, March 28, 1890, p. 4, c. 4 (reprinted from the Washington [La.] *Advertiser*).
50 New Orleans *Picayune*, February 22, 1890, p. 4, c. 3.
51 Interview with Avery "Kid" Howard, May 22, 1961, pp. 12–13, in William Ransom Hogan Jazz Archive, Howard-Tilton Memorial Library, Tulane University, New Orleans.
52 Bocage interview, February 6, 1962, p. 7, in Hogan Jazz Archive.
53 Interview with Jack "Papa" Laine, March 26, 1957, p. 1, in William Ransom Hogan Jazz Archive, Howard-Tilton Memorial Library, Tulane University, New Orleans. Another Laine alumnus, Raymond Lopez, recalled his first brass band job, *ca.* 1910, a Holy Name church parade for which Laine furnished around *ten* 10-piece bands. Lopez recalled that they played *by ear* such marches as "The Washington Post," "Semper Fidelis" and "The American Soldier (Bugle Boy) March." Interview with Raymond Lopez, October 30, 1958, pp. 9–11, in William Ransom Hogan Jazz Archive, Howard-Tilton Memorial Library, Tulane University, New Orleans. This is corroborated by Fred Guarante, a white New Orleans musician who went North to big-time dance band work. He described "[G. B.] Mars' Brass Band, which used to 'swing' their band numbers in syncopated rhythm style when on parade through the streets of New Orleans." Paul

M. Specht, *How They Became Name Bands* (New York: Fine Arts Publishers, 1941), 105.

54 Laine interview, May 23, 1960, p. 7, in Hogan Jazz Archive.

55 Laine interview, March 26, 1957, p. 19, *ibid.*

56 *Ibid.*, 7.

57 Interview with Johnny Lala, September 24, 1958, p. 1, in William Ransom Hogan Jazz Archive, Howard-Tilton Memorial Library, Tulane University, New Orleans.

58 *Ibid.*, 22.

59 Interview with Arthur "Monk" Hazel, July 16, 1959, p. 1, in William Ransom Hogan Jazz Archive, Howard-Tilton Memorial Library, Tulane University, New Orleans.

60 Henry interview, January 8, 1959, p. 29, in Hogan Jazz Archive.

Chapter Two

1 New Orleans *Picayune*, August 2, 1838, p. 2, c. 1.

2 Bocage interview, January 29, 1959, pp. 49–50, in Hogan Jazz Archive.

3 William Russell's *Notes* (1945), 417–18, in William Ransom Hogan Jazz Archive, Howard-Tilton Memorial Library, Tulane University, New Orleans.

4 The *Jazz at Ohio Union* concert has been issued by the following record companies: Disc Jockey DJL 100; Pax 9003/9004; Dan (Japanese) VC-8001/8002.

5 The best example of Matthews' work is with a group under his own name issued on *Music of New Orleans*, Good Time Jazz 12019.

6 *E.g.*, this announcement in a social column of a black newspaper: "The Alliance Brass Band will give a grand fancy dress and calico ball on Nov. 4th, at the Globe's Hall." New Orleans *Weekly Pelican*, October 5, 1889, p. 3, c. 1.

7 The quadrille was a kind of cultivated "square dance" incorporating a series (usually five) of dances, each with a characteristic step calling for a special music. The five sections contrasted with each other and were usually in 6/8 and 2/4 meters. Its popularity in New Orleans, with the prominent French culture, lasted past the turn of the century.

8 Lomax, *Mister Jelly Roll*, 66.

9 Edmond Souchon, "King Oliver: A Very Personal Memoir," in Martin Williams (ed.), *Jazz Panorama* (New York: Collier Books, 1964), 28.

10 For a discussion of the adaptation of the tune into New Orleans jazz, see William J. Schafer, "Breaking into 'High Society': Musical Metamorphoses in Early Jazz," *Journal of Jazz Studies*, II (June, 1975), 53–60.

11 Marches in 6/8 combine the feeling of double- and triple-meter music. The signature is sometimes called "compound duple meter," because it stresses a main 1-2 pattern by subdividing, yet the two halves of a measure also divide into patterns of threes, so that rhythmic figures ♪♪♪ or ♩ ♪ recur. This creates a tension between the 1–2 of dotted quarter notes (♩. ♩.) and the three-grouped eighth notes (♪♪♪ ♪♪♪), almost like polyrhythmic music.

12 Reported in Samuel B. Charters, *Jazz: New Orleans, 1885–1957* (Belleville, N.J.: Walter C. Allen, 1958), 44.

13 Nat Hentoff, "Jazz in the Twenties: Garvin Bushell," in Williams (ed.), *Jazz Panorama*, 77–78.

14 *Ibid.*, 72.

15 Many New Orleans jazzmen traveled regularly with tent shows of various kinds; among the more famous were Bunk Johnson and Ernest "Kid Punch" Miller and, more recently, Worthia G. "Show Boy" Thomas.

16 Henry A. Kmen, "The Music of New Orleans," in Hodding Carter (ed.), *The Past as Prelude: New Orleans, 1718–1968* (New Orleans: Tulane University, 1968), 231–32.

17 See the two recordings of "Panama" by the Eureka Brass Band on *Music of the Eureka Brass Band*, Folkways FA 2462, and on *The Eureka Brass Band*, Atlantic 1408, and the recording of it by the Young Tuxedo Brass Band on *Jazz Begins*, Atlantic 1297.

18 See "Whoopin' Blues" by the Eureka Brass Band, on *The Eureka Brass Band*, Atlantic 1408, and "John Casimir's Whoopin' Blues" by the Young Tuxedo Brass Band, on *Jazz Begins*, Atlantic 1297.

19 Willie Parker, a founding member of the Eureka Brass Band, related the story of naming an earlier band he helped to organize: "Me, I got that name [Terminal Brass Band]; we made up a brass band from the orchestra, you know. . . . So everybody had to bring a name. And I happened to go up Canal Street, to the depot there—they tored it up now—Basin and Canal. Well, they had 'Terminal' marked up on there. 'Oh,' I say, 'that's a good name, I'm going to carry it to the band.' And I carried it to the band and they accept it. Everybody was to bring a name for the band; we was just organizing the band." Interview with Willie Parker, November 7, 1958, p. 43, in William Ransom Hogan Jazz Archive, Howard-Tilton Memorial Library, Tulane University, New Orleans.

20 New Orleans *Weekly Pelican*, December 25, 1886, p. 3, c. 1.
21 *Woods Directory*, 16–17. Also listed under "Bands and Orchestras" is an entry for "Excelsior Brass Band & Orchestra, Geo. Moret, Leader," 15.
22 New Orleans *Item*, March 20, 1901, p. 1, c. 2.
23 New Orleans *Weekly Pelican*, August 27, 1887, p. 3, c. 1: "There will be a grand broom drill by the Eureka Guards. Music by the Onward Band."
24 New Orleans *Weekly Pelican*, January 15, 1887, p. 3, c. 1.
25 An early chronicler of black composers and musicians in the nineteenth century records the existence of black brass bands named "Excelsior" in both Boston and Philadelphia during the 1870s. See Trotter, *Music and Some Highly Musical People*, 294, 309. In relating the story of an early black brass band, "Frank Johnson's Band" of Philadelphia, Trotter gives us a vivid eyewitness account of a parade: "This writer well remembers when in 1852, on 'St. John's Day,' this fine corps of musicians came to Cincinnati. With ranks so deployed as to almost extend across Broadway Street, they moved in most soldierly manner up the same at the head of a Masonic order, playing indeed most 'soul-animating strains,' and winning the while the warm admiration of a vast throng of people that lined the sidewalks," 309.
26 Louis Armstrong recalled the ceremonial feelings of brass bandsmen: "And the musicians always have their uniforms on —a little music lyre on the collar around their neck, and the band's name on the hat. The bands wanted to be stipulated, you know . . ." See Richard Meryman, *Louis Armstrong—A Self-Portrait* (New York: Eakins Press, 1971), 11.
27 Advertisement for Victor Records, New Orleans *Item*, May 11, 1917, p. 7, c. 1–3.
28 William Russell's *Notes* (1945), 672, in Hogan Jazz Archives.
29 For a photograph and description of the WPA band, see Al Rose and Edmond Souchon, *New Orleans Jazz: A Family Album* (Baton Rouge: Louisiana State University Press, 1967), 184.
30 Charles Edward Smith, "New Orleans and Traditions in Jazz," in Nat Hentoff and Albert McCarthy (eds.), *Jazz* (New York: Grove Press, 1961), 21–41.
31 *Ibid.*, 33.
32 Bocage expressed bitterness about the fading of reading traditions in the brass bands, as compared to bands of his youth: "It wasn't quite as bad as it is today, you know; it was a little better, because they used to use a bit more music than they use today. But now, you go out there today, you don't play no music at all, outside of funeral, funeral march, that's all." Bocage interview, January 24, 1959, p. 53, in Hogan Jazz Archive. Bocage's

playing is heard to best advantage on *Peter Bocage*, Riverside RLP 379, or in his early recordings with Piron's New Orleans Orchestra, three selections of which are included on *New Orleans Jazz: The Twenties*, RBF 203.
33 As noted, Percy Humphrey, leader of the Eureka band, had connections with the brass-band tradition going back as far as his grandfather, James Humphrey of Magnolia plantation. The manager of the Eureka band, Joseph "Red" Clark, also had a long family history in brass bandsmanship. His father, Aaron Clark, was a baritone horn player with the old Onward Brass Band in the 1880s and also played with the Excelsior Brass Band and the Pickwick Brass Band. Interview with Joseph "Red" Clark, January 13, 1959, p. 1, in William Ransom Hogan Jazz Archive, Howard-Tilton Memorial Library, Tulane University, New Orleans.

Chapter Three

1 Illustrating the use of hymns by military bands in nineteenth-century memorial processions, a brief news item relates that the Washington Artillery Band played a rendition of "In the Sweet Bye and Bye" for ceremonies dedicating the Washington Artillery Monument. See New Orleans *Daily States*, February 21, 1880, p. 2, c. 3.
2 Lyle Saxon *et al.*, *Gumbo Ya Ya* (Boston: Houghton Mifflin, 1945), 66.
3 Laine interview, May 23, 1960, p. 7, and Lopez interview, August 30, 1958, p. 17, both in Hogan Jazz Archive.
4 Lala interview, September 24, 1958, pp. 17–18, *ibid.*
5 Clark interview, November 11, 1959, pp. 14, 5, *ibid.* Clark cited as the kind of marches the Eureka band would choose such standards as "The Stars and Stripes Forever," "National Emblem," "Under Fire," "Under Arms," and "Rifle Rangers." He also mentioned "Oh, Didn't He Ramble?" and "Gettysburg March" as old favorites for the return from the cemetery that had almost disappeared from the bands' repertoires.
6 William Russell's *Notes* (1945), 812–14, in Hogan Jazz Archive.
7 See recordings of "Garlands of Flowers" by the Eureka Brass Band, which interpolates a rendition of "Just a Closer Walk with Thee," and of "Medley of Hymns" by the Young Tuxedo Brass Band, which synthesizes two formal dirges and a standard hymn into one piece of funeral music.
8 The most succinct expression of this concept of heterophonic improvisational style is in William Russell's notes to "George Lewis and His New Orleans Stompers," Blue Note LP 1206, Vol. 2:

Trumpet, clarinet, and trombone all play concurrently different versions of the same melody, rather than counter melodies or accompanying figures. Each is saying exactly the same thing, but in a different manner, in his own characteristic instrumental language. The trumpet plays in a decisive, full-toned, driving style; the trombone more brusquely accented, smeary, and with greater economy as befits a heavier horn, while the clarinet embellishes the tune more elaborately but nonetheless still sings the theme. . . . Thus New Orleans ensemble often consists of several instruments playing solos simultaneously, and the result, rather than a polyphony, is a heterophony more related to certain Oriental musics than to European.

9 Transcribed by the author, with occasional minor omissions, from the *Baby Dodds Talking Record*, American Music BD–1.

10 See also the recorded memoirs of Jelly Roll Morton, Library of Congress session, and Bunk Johnson's reminiscences on Good Time Jazz and American Music recordings for this spontaneous bardic style.

11 Larry Gara, *The Baby Dodds Story* (Los Angeles: Contemporary Press, 1959), 17–18.

12 Henry interview, October 21, 1959, p. 14, in Hogan Jazz Archive.

13 *Ibid.*, 25–26.

14 *Ibid.*

15 Clark interview, 8–9, in Hogan Jazz Archive.

16 *Ibid.*, 14.

17 See Eureka Brass Band file, entry for January 28, 1963, in William Ransom Hogan Jazz Archive, Howard-Tilton Memorial Library, Tulane University, New Orleans.

18 *Ibid.*, entry for April 5, 1960.

19 Whitney Balliett, *Such Sweet Thunder* (Indianapolis: Bobbs-Merrill, 1966), 332–34.

20 Hazel interview, June 16, 1959, p. 3, and Lala interview, September 24, 1958, pp.11–12, both in Hogan Jazz Archive.

21 Bunk Johnson maintained that Joe Oliver first gained his New Orleans reputation and following only after he went with Manuel Perez and played with the Onward Brass Band in the streets: see Frederic Ramsey, Jr., and Charles Edward Smith, *Jazzmen* (New York: Harcourt, Brace and Co., 1939), 61.

22 See Interviews with Ernest Burden "Kid Punch" Miller, August 20, 1959, and August 23, 1960, in William Ransom Hogan Jazz Archive, Howard-Tilton Memorial Library, Tulane University, New Orleans.

23 There is a stirring performance of the march by the Six and Seven-Eighths String Band on *The Six and Seven-Eighths String Band of New Orleans*, Folkways FP 671.

24 On the Library of Congress recordings, *Boyhood Memories*, Vol. 1, Riverside RLP 9001.

25 Many non–New Orleans musicians learned with brass bands and were taught through brass-band methods in all parts of the country. See interview with George Mitchell, June 1, 1959, p. 1, in William Ransom Hogan Jazz Archive, Howard-Tilton Memorial Library, Tulane University, New Orleans. The background of a great swing trumpeter is explained as follows: "A Georgetown police officer (J. Arthur Johnson) started a boys' band and succeeded in becoming responsible for Rex's musical education. Rex [Stewart] began his career on a bass cornet and was promoted to regular cornet within a few months. Before the police officer's death, he became first cornetist. Those three years constitute Rex's true musical training. The band played in concerts, parades and churches." Rex Stewart, *Jazz Masters of the Thirties* (New York: Macmillan, 1972), 213.

26 Saxon *et al.*, *Gumbo Ya Ya*, 3–9.

Index